The Leisurely Route to the Med

By John Hartley and Pauline Drury

*From England to Gibraltar
and beyond following the coastal route*

Acknowledgements

WE WOULD like to thank all the people who made the voyage and book possible, and the many experienced sailors whose advice we received about various aspects of the voyage. Derek Williams installed most of the extra equipment we needed, and also gave us plenty of advice from his own experience in the Med. Gavin Hearnden of Mount Batten Boathouse was most helpful in providing the spares and equipment we needed. Robin Blain of Sunbird Marine has always been ready to give advice on any aspect of the junk rig.

Jon Stevens sailed with us from Plymouth to Bilbao, and his sailing experience and knowledge of the French coast were a decided asset.

The illustrations are from various sources. We gratefully acknowledge that: the photographs of *Zefka* were taken by John Moulton; the illustrations: 9, Santander; 13 Ribadeo; 17 La Coruña, and 22 Bayona are the copyright of the Spanish Tourist Office and are included with permission; and 23, Viana do Costelo, 25 Torre de Belem, 27 Lisbon square, 29 Lagos, and 30 the Algarve are copyright of the Portuguese Tourist Office and are reproduced with permission. Our thanks also to the Gibraltar Tourist Board for illustration 30. The aerial view of Belle Île is reprinted with permission from Editions D'Art Jos Le Doaré.

Foreword

THERE are three ways of getting to the Med in a small boat: you can chug across France strung about with fenders; turn hard a'port at Ushant and outside-all to Gib; or you can follow the coastal route of the Phoenicians.

Many people are wary of coasting the western fringes of Europe. Perhaps it is an age-old dread of the lee shore. The howling winter storms of nor'west Brittany and the ominous gape of Biscay's awesome bay spread little cheer among Nelson's blockading fleets and merchant seamen alike.

This book puts such fears into perspective. The writers are no hairy Cape Horn die-hards, they are a couple of typical, moderately experienced but conscientious sailors, who can get sick and scared like anybody else. Their account of port hopping south is a very contemporary and extremely detailed one, invaluable to any who follow. In times past they would have dwelt mainly on anchorages, holding grounds and shelter. Instead and more appropriately they assess marinas, amenities and—give an *Egon Ronay* style run-down on showers and loos!

Short stages meant that they avoided many night hazards of the northerly Portugese Trades and the dead run in huge seas (make sure that all crew can run with confidence). Also the scary appearance out of the darkness ahead of twenty-foot fishing markers.

Fishing boats dash around at great speed, behaving in a bewildering fashion which can be worrying at night. It pays to find out all you can about their methods. If you berth in a Spanish fishing port don't leave or enter around midnight on a Sunday. At a minute past twelve, religious scruples and thirsts satisfied, crews cast off and go whooping seaward three abreast!

Des Sleightholme

Introduction

BEFORE we set out for the Mediterranean, we were basically weekend sailors who enjoyed our cruising. The longest holiday we had had aboard was when we sailed from Plymouth to and around the Channel Islands and back the previous summer. That involved a distance of 250 miles and about ten days; we were now about to embark on a voyage of over 1,500 miles.

Our experiences show that with good preparation and reasonable caution, any couple who enjoy sailing can have a wonderful time on a voyage to the Med. Of course, we had our problems, but these are all part of sailing!

Part of our preparation involved driving through France, Spain and Portugal, looking at some of the marinas and rias. However, that was not strictly necessary, and certainly once you've read this book you won't need to do it.

Although most of the book is written from the skipper's viewpoint, we both wrote and edited parts throughout the book.

Pauline Drury
John Hartley

Chapter One

The Dream and The Grand Plan

EVER SINCE I started sailing yachts in 1989, I have dreamed of sailing somewhere warm like the Mediterranean. Much as I enjoy sailing along the English coast, cold weather—even in the summer—damps my enthusiasm. My partner Pauline suffers even more from the cold so, once she was able to sail regularly, we knew we had to sail to the Med.

By taking the most direct route, and sailing day and night, it is possible to complete the trip in about two weeks. But it's hard going! Our idea was to have fun and adventure without boredom, fear and danger. To us this meant following the French and North Spanish coasts rather than heading straight across the Bay of Biscay. We needed around two months to do it our way and once in the Med we wanted to be able to go for extended cruising holidays. So, because we are still working, we had to reorganise our lives to enable us to get away for one or two months at a time. Only then could we turn the dream into reality.

The Leisurely Route to the Med

When I sold the MacWester Wight 30-foot ketch I had sailed for nine years, we started to look for a suitable boat. This was not easy because I wanted a boat with a modern junk rig and one which was suitable to sail to and around the Mediterranean. As is usually the case, almost all the suitable boats seemed much too expensive.

It took us about six months to find and buy *Zefka*, a Brewer 33 junk rig schooner that had been equipped with the most modern Superjunk rig and undergone a major refit. *Zefka* has an aluminium hull and was built with junk rig sails in Canada specially for long-distance cruising for two. She had crossed the Atlantic and been sailed in the Mediterranean by its first owners, and so was obviously suitable. Details of the specification of *Zefka* are shown in the second section of the book. We had her brought down from Hartlepool to Plymouth by road in January, and then our preparation for the voyage began.

In the first year, we had a few changes made and sailed as often as the weather allowed so that we could learn how to handle *Zefka*. Like most boats, she does not always do what you expect, especially when going astern, and there was the added complication that we were novices with any junk rig, let alone a schooner.

I think we made every mistake possible in the learning process—ropes tied themselves in knots, got entangled with each other, around the life raft and the Dorade vents. On more than one occasion, the main halyard looped itself around the kedge anchor which is mounted on the side of the pulpit. Once we set the foresail too low and the boom got under the pulpit when we reefed. However, so forgiving is the junk rig that we still managed to sail where we wanted to when we wanted to, and never had any serious problems. And we learned how not to do these things.

Not everything we had to learn was connected with the rig. We had observed that the compass reading on the display panel for the automatic pilot seemed to tally pretty well with that of the boat's compass, which was partly obscured by the folded sprayhood—it is mounted on gimbals just forward of the main hatch. So when we were on course from Falmouth to Plymouth one day, we set the course by the automatic pilot. That turned out to be a big mistake, as we discovered when we found we were heading directly for the Eddystone lighthouse, which is about ten miles off

The Dream and The Grand Plan

Plymouth! Following that incident, we made sure the main compass was always visible, and completely ignored the reading on the automatic pilot display.

By the end of the season, which included a five-day cruise to the Falmouth area and a ten-day cruise to the Channel Islands, we knew we had a very seaworthy boat that sailed really well. Just what we needed for our trip to the Med! All we had to do was to prepare ourselves and the boat—quite daunting. But we set our target date and cancelled *Zefka's* permanent mooring, so now we were visitors and had to go.

From March onward, we were frenetically working on the boat, buying and studying charts, organising provisions, and at the same time I was busy doing five months' normal work in three months. We had some new sail covers made, and a simple mains electricity system was installed so that we could use the electricity that is normally included on the Continent in marina fees. Among the bigger jobs we did was to fit stiffer battens in the foresail and to make some awnings and start on a bimini.

There is always some panic in preparations for such a voyage as this. It is best to expect it, although of course like most people, we did not. We had spent so much time working on the boat that we hardly sailed at all, but knew that we had to test the rig and practice anchoring. *Zefka* has a large anchor and an electric windlass, which we needed to learn how to use.

Eventually, we found time to sail around Plymouth Sound for a trial. All was well until we went outside the breakwater where there was quite a swell. Every time we went over a wave, we could hear a sort of 'clonk'. It was pretty clear that the rudder was bouncing up and down on its support.

When we got in I asked Derek Williams, a marine engineer and friend to take a look at it and his verdict was simple:

'I wouldn't go sailing far with that. Either the rudder is loose on the stock or there is a problem with the bottom bearing.'

Obviously, we had to get that fixed. *Zefka* came out of the water, and we lowered the rudder. The rudder and stock turned out to be a one-piece fabrication, but the bottom bearing was turning in the stock. Fortunately, Haggert Commerial Marine was able to sort the problem out in a couple of days, and once again we went out for a trial sail. All went well. *Zefka* was ready; were we?

The Leisurely Route to the Med

Pauline had been gathering a large quantity of provisions for our two-month voyage. Although we had no plans to stay at sea for more than a couple of days, we took most of our basic food so that we would need to buy fruit and vegetables only when in port, and thus save some time. We are both committed vegetarians—we don't eat any animal products including milk—and we knew it would probably be difficult to obtain some of our requirements, such as soya milk. We thought that the mountain of clothes for all weather, food, household provisions and spare yacht parts would not fit into the boat, but we actually had empty storage spaces when everything was stowed.

Now the Grand Plan was being worked out. For the first leg of the voyage we were to have an extra crew member, Jon Stevens. Jon is an old sailing friend, and an accomplished sailor. We had both started to sail in Guernsey about nine years previously. Since then Jon has sailed his 23-foot Gypsy II through the canals to Spain and sailed around the Balearics for four years. He was keen to get a decent voyage in that year, which was good for us as our insurance company preferred that we had a crew of three across the Bay of Biscay.

As recommended by some experienced sailors, we were to start the voyage by sailing from Plymouth to Falmouth. There are several reasons for this as outlined in Chapter 15. An added advantage for us was that Jon would be able to gain some experience of the junk rig before we crossed the channel.

The channel crossing itself is straightforward, but you need to time the departure so that you arrive at the entrance to the Chenal du Four just as the strong tidal flow turns south. I decided to play safe, and start so that if we made better progress than expected we would arrive a little too early. There is a further channel, Raz de Sein, where timing is critical, and this would be on route the following day.

Once along the French coast, we planned to take our time. We had no intention of dashing across in the quickest manner possible, which would involve several days at sea without stopping. No, we were planning to hop along the coast, to stop in some of the beautiful French harbours and anchorages, and then cruise into rather than past the exciting rias of northern Spain.

The Dream and The Grand Plan

In other words, we wanted to make sure we would have 'time to smell the primroses on the way', as the great golfer, Bobby Jones said. Even so, we knew this would be a real adventure. Now we were going to turn the Dream into Reality, and that was the Grand Plan. The question was how far would we get?

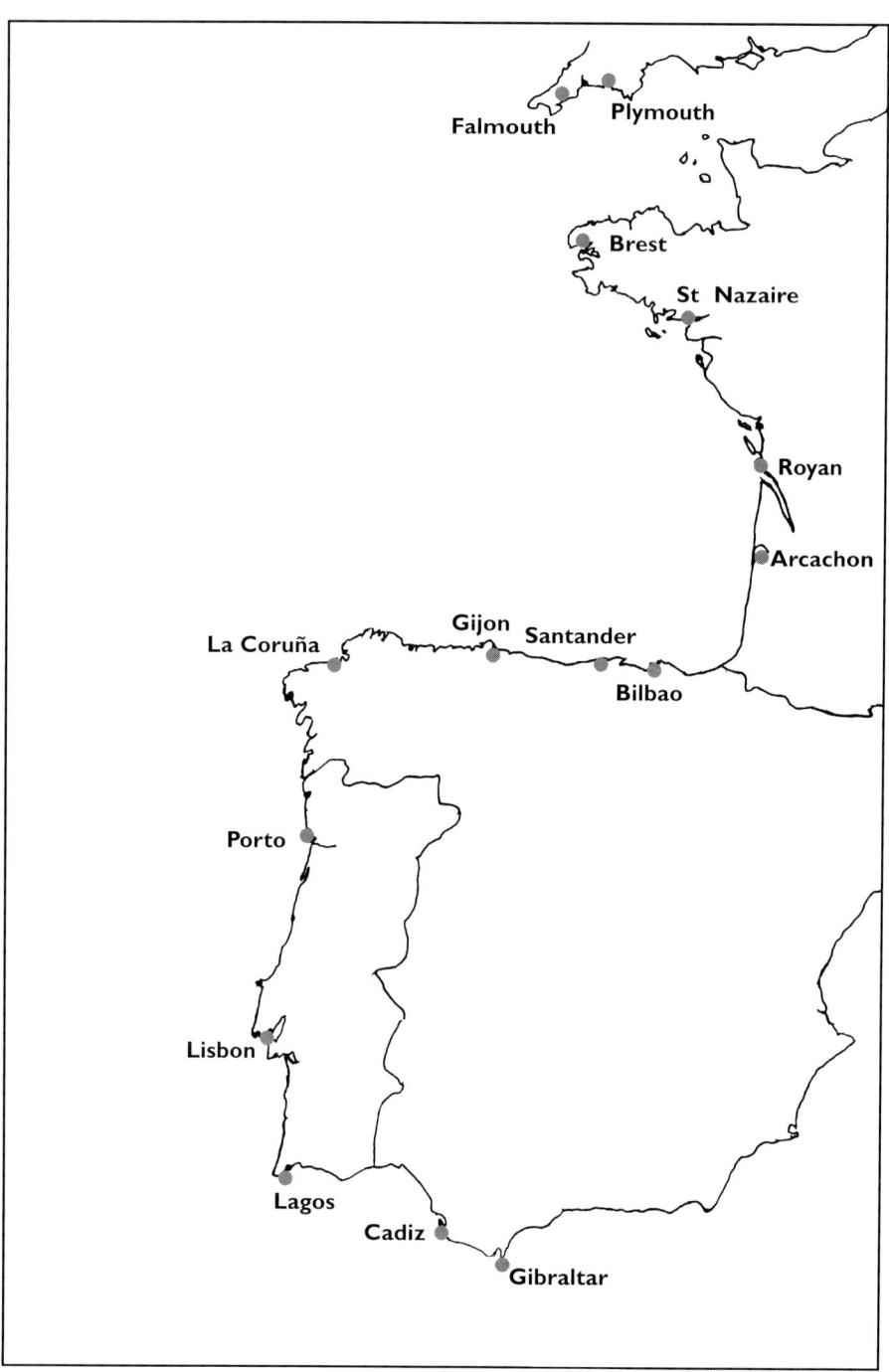

Chapter Two

The cold channel and the warmth of Concarneau

6th June: Not a good start. Our early enthusiasm gave way to sogginess as heavy rain set in.

A GALE caused us to delay our departure by a day, and when we awoke we were cheered by the clear skies, despite the chill in the air. We set off full of enthusiasm, but before long light rain fell. After a couple of hours or so of fighting a headwind and a swell left over from the gale, the rain intensified and progress was so slow that we turned into Fowey instead of going on to Falmouth.

There we saw *Colin Hannah*, a 35-foot steel sloop, on the next buoy. We had learned only the previous day that the young couple who owned her were leaving Plymouth Yacht Haven for the Med on the same day as us, intent on following a similar route. In fact, they had left about an hour earlier.

The Leisurely Route to the Med

7th June: Wind good deal stronger than the forecast. Trying to find our sea legs!

Our spirits were raised the next morning by a good weather forecast: a north-westerly of force three to four, which would give us a following wind all the way, although they did mention some stronger gusts. An almost ideal wind for the crossing.

So we abandoned all thought of going to Falmouth and headed directly across the channel for Camaret. We set off under full sail, and with the sun breaking through from time to time, all was well. Less than an hour after we left, a squall blew up and we had to reef down, and still shot along at around seven knots. The squall soon passed over and we shook out the reefs. Not much later we saw another squall coming, but this one turned out to be stronger, so after a while we were down to just three of the seven panels in each sail, and were still corkscrewing over the swell at around six knots. This time the wind did not diminish; the squall turned into a strong wind, with some stronger gusts, that was to push us across the Channel, maintaining that sort of speed throughout the day and night. We just accepted this as normal and got into the rhythm of sailing. Gradually, the swell increased during the day and as it was coming from the rear quarter the motion was quite uncomfortable. At least it wasn't raining!

We discovered afterwards that we were crossing in a force six, the sort of weather which we normally sit out, in the harbour or at home. After all, we are not long-distance mariners but basically weekend and summer holiday sailors. Nevertheless, tackling much stronger winds than had been forecast—usually for relatively short periods—was to become commonplace. Despite the sunshine, it was a very cold day for June. By the late afternoon I started to feel cold, and by the evening was feeling awful. Weeks of preparation, the tension caused by the odd crisis, and the need to finish a mountain of office work before we left were catching up with me. Also, I had forgotten one of the golden rules of sailing. When you say to yourself: 'I'm cold, better get some more clothes,' that is the time to do it. I did not put warm clothes on until dark by which time, much to my annoyance, I had been seasick.

Pauline wrote in her diary: 'After several hours of corkscrewing, I realised that Sea Bands were not going to be sufficient and quickly swallowed two Stugeron. Usually John is the one who can cope with navigating and preparing meals below without ill effects, so he thought he would be all right. It was good that Jon Stevens could now take control while our skipper rested and recovered his strength.'

Nothing like getting a bad experience out of the way early on—or so I hoped.

Some of the waves were long and deep. Jon, always ready with a quip, christened them 'real baskets' as the first one hurled the fruit basket off its fiddled shelf sending apples, oranges and kiwis rolling around the floor. Pauline continues the tale of the night:

'The rough seas made it extremely difficult even to make hot drinks—it was possible only if you put the mugs in the sink, and then most of the boiling water missed and went down the plug hole! Opening the sliding cupboard doors to get out mugs and coffee was fraught with difficulties because Marmite, biscuits and mustard came flying out as the boat rolled, and the contents which remained in the cupboard piled themselves up against the doors so that they would neither open nor close.'

At this stage, Pauline was beginning to wonder whether this was the voyage to the sun she had promised herself. She writes:

'Even with a hot drink inside me it was difficult to keep warm and I was wearing seven layers! Could it really be June? Was this voyage really going to be better than remaining at home or even going to work? '

'We had made such good time during the day that during the night Jon realised we would arrive at Chenal du Four several hours too early, so we turned south-west, which improved the motion of the boat and slowed us down. For about an hour we hardly moved toward the destination at all but the wind blew hard throughout the night, and the speed of the water passing the hull gave the impression of moving forward at a good speed. It was a beautiful starry night above and, as we watched the bow waves, we could see tiny stars of twinkling lights in the water below—phosphorescence produced by millions of tiny creatures as we disturbed their world. How silly to think we were alone out there when the water around us was teaming with life.'

The Leisurely Route to the Med

'Several ships passed by in the distance, their directions apparent from the position of their lights. Near dawn a fulmar joined us, flying a few yards off the stern. Two more of these large birds appeared briefly—three black silhouettes against the grey sky. Then with a tilt of their wings they were gone.'

After dawn the wind slackened a little, and we crossed the shipping lanes, which separate ships travelling west from those going east. Fortunately, visibility was good, and all the ships we saw were some distance away, so they did not present any problems—they just helped us keep alert.

The swell continued much the same until we reached the Chenal du Four, where the islands afford some protection; indeed, that is the main reason why small boats go inside the islands rather than out in the open sea. The other reason is that outside you have to mix it with large ships which is always best avoided.

8th June: Sighted land early, and in the afternoon the sun was warming our backs. Fun with the Customs men before it rained.

We sighted land in the form of the flat Île d'Ouessant at 08:13 after sailing for 102 miles, and a couple of hours later entered the Chenal du Four a little earlier than planned. It was virtually slack water, and here the sea was much flatter which made life more enjoyable.

The current was running at about three knots at its fastest that day, instead of the five knots you can get, because it was a neap tide. On the chart the Chenal looks pretty difficult. There seem to be rocks strewn all around, and to avoid them you need to change direction several times. In fact it is simple enough, thanks largely to the wonderful French lighthouses and beacons. The lighthouses are tall towers, often 50 metres high, which can be seen for miles. In many places, there are two lighthouses, a newer one built alongside the old one, and these make marvellous landmarks. Buoys in British waters are often small and leaning with the wind or tide while beacons may be little more than sticks. Not so in France! Even the beacons are usually solid towers 10-20 metres high. And so it was in the Chenal du Four. Therefore, it was easy to keep in the deep channel, and we soon realised that not only is the Chenal easy to find, but it is very wide. In some areas you do not strictly need to stick to the marked passage; we did, however.

The cold channel and the warmth of Concarneau

Eventually we came out into the Rade de Brest. Although there was a slight swell, it was pretty gentle and the wind was from the west. The Rade is a wide estuary with green hills and cliffs on either side. It felt warm and welcoming after the grey morning in the Chenal du Four. We set our course for the Charles Martel buoy in the middle of the channel and slackened off the sheets to sail almost downwind. After a few moments, the foresail lazily swung across so that we goose winged almost silently with *Zefka's* magnificent tan sails a sight to behold. One of the joys of a junk-rig schooner is that downwind it goose wings easily in a very stable manner. If the wind shifts the foresail may gybe, but because everything is so light it is quite harmless.

So, in good spirits, with some warmth on our backs we sailed upstream until, at around half past two, we passed the headland behind which Camaret hides from the westerly winds. You need to go up as far as the Swansea Vale buoy—presumably named after a ship that sunk nearby—in the channel off the headland before turning into the bay. As we took the sails down and headed for the breakwater in the distance it looked as if we had come to a beautifully calm refuge.

We were not disappointed: there were plenty of pontoons, but without any fingers, so the six or so boats in the marina were moored side-on. They were almost all British. We headed for the first empty pontoon, and moored right at the end; keep it simple seemed like a good motto at the time. It was now 3.50pm, 30 hours since we left Fowey and we had covered 135 miles. It had been quite a baptism of fire for all of us, just one more routine voyage for *Zefka*. As we busied ourselves fitting the sail covers and adjusting the warps, a yacht of about 38 feet arrived almost opposite us. Then we heard the skipper shout:

'For God's sake, you should know which is the stern warp! You've been sailing for 27 years.' This was addressed to his obviously long-suffering wife.

Pauline remarked indignantly: 'I know just where I'd put his stupid rope if he spoke to me like that.'

She adds: 'Why is it that some men encourage their wives to participate in their hobby—or passion—and then find it necessary to hurl abuse at them because they aren't able to pull in a sheet in a howling gale or temporarily confuse port and starboard? Women beware! Consider this possibility and eliminate it before embarking on a voyage to the Med with your beloved!'

We just hoped that their sailing holiday improved or that the berated wife transferred to their friend's yacht on the next berth leaving him to cope single-handed. Actually, this turned out to be an isolated example of male chauvinism; thereafter we saw harmony among most of the couples around.

After that little drama, we were still adjusting things when a large inflatable launch entered the harbour and moored opposite *Zefka*. Two men and a woman were aboard. After mooring the vessel, the men stood around and looked at us, while the woman walked off up the pontoon. Then, we noticed that their oilies were actually uniforms with the legend 'Douane' on their sleeves.

They produced a long form, and took our details in a pretty light-hearted way. In fact, the man who filled the form in did not seem to know where everything went and kept asking his colleague. Eventually, the form was complete, and he gave us a little certificate which he said we should show to any other customs officer who approached us, and thus avoid any formalities again. A useful piece of information. By now it was quite cold and grey, and I remarked on the weather.

The officer asked where we were heading and I told him we were going south. He said:

'You will find the weather is much warmer in South Brittany than here. The whole weather pattern is completely different. You will like Concarneau. It is a much nicer place than Camaret. I was born there.'

As the drizzle turned to steady, cold rain we hoped he was right. We went ashore looking forward to a good hot shower and a drink in a French café. As a regular stopping port for yachts crossing the channel, we assumed it was bound to have good facilities, a welcoming yacht club and handy telephones for calming families' fears that you might not make it across the channel. Dream on! The marina office was closed and deserted. The new toilet and shower block was a long walk in the rain, beyond the large basin for local yachts and fishing boats. Only then did we discover that *jetons* were needed to obtain hot water and, you've guessed it, only obtainable from the marina office! The telephone nearby sullenly refused to accept coins or credit cards; phone cards must be purchased from the town, further than we were prepared to walk in the rain. However we did find a café, part of a tourist hotel, where we were able to enjoy that relaxing drink before returning to the boat for a relay of showers using our adequate, but rather cramped, facilities on board. That evening, June or not, we lit the diesel heater to warm our bones and dry out the boat after all the ablutions.

Although we did not explore Camaret further there is certainly not much to recommend it in June. However, it is a superb haven, well sheltered from the wind and swell, and must be more pleasant than the vast marina at Brest which has one bar only and is really a huge boat park. In any case, Brest is much further off your route than Camaret.

9th June: Warm sunshine and light winds through the Raz de Sein to Audierne

By the next morning it had stopped raining and the sun was making an effort to come through, so life seemed a lot better. Our next port of call was to be dictated by the need to arrive at the Raz de Sein, some 20 miles from Camaret, when the current was flowing south. Since that meant a mid-morning start, we decided to go to Audierne as that would give us a reasonable passage the following day to Concarneau or Benodet. We left at about 10am aiming to reach the Raz de Sein, the passage inside the Île de Sein, when the flow was starting to turn south at about 1.30pm.

As we left the marina, Pauline got out her new camcorder, and filmed the view. She explains:

'I had always felt rather disparagingly about people I saw wearing their camcorders like extra appendages and filming their loved ones as they exclaim over waterfalls, walk up cathedral steps or sip piña coladas, or whatever, in the setting sun. That was all before I acquired *my* camcorder! It is a JVC VHS-C type which has cassettes that can be put in an adapter of a standard VCR and viewed straight away. You can't do this with an 8mm camcorder. So I was able to post filmed cassettes to my parents who are no longer able to travel. During the whole voyage I filmed a total of five and a half hours on eight tapes and sent them back—the first one from Les Sables d'Olonne. The videos were much enjoyed, although there were some complaints about feeling seasick at times while watching them.'

The Leisurely Route to the Med

We sailed off in company with three other British boats intent on arriving at Le Raz de Sein at about the same time. As we left we noticed *Harrier,* which had been in Plymouth Yacht Haven the day before we left, but no sign of *Colin Hannah*; nor did we see her again. However, we heard later that in the beginning of August the skipper had phoned from somewhere in Portugal with a problem with the auto pilot steering gear. Outside the harbour, the sea was calm and we set off around the headland in weak sunshine. The wind was light as we motor-sailed for the first hour or so. Here the rugged coast was interesting with islands of large, jagged rocks rising out of the sea. Probably, because of our experience of sailing around the Channel Islands, we expected the deep water through the Raz de Sein to be about as wide in places as a decent river, but when we approached we realised that again the factor of scale had played tricks on us. It is actually very wide, and there is plenty of room to work out the direction of the channel as you go. With some help from the current we wooshed through the Raz, and then headed a little closer to the shore so that we would be able to find Audierne; on the chart, it appeared to be a very small inlet.

The coast in this area is very pleasant. Long sandy beaches and fairly flat hinterland with low green hills behind. With the light airs, *Zefka* was gliding along gently, and eventually we found what we thought must be the entrance to Audierne. It is rather an unusual place in that there is a bay with a breakwater across two-thirds of its width, and this is the main shelter. You can pick up a buoy or anchor there, but it is about half a mile from the entrance to the river, and of course further still from the town. Alternatively, you can motor up the river a mile or so to a small marina; but to do so you need to arrive within three hours of high water.

Well, we arrived at about one hour after high water, so it was worth going up river to the town. The passage is quite narrow and, in theory, well marked, although some of the marks are not where you might expect them. So with Jon at the helm, we entered the river keeping close to the jetty that runs out at right angles to the land. The water was only about three metres deep. Then, you turn through 15 degrees and a pair of white boards with red chevrons need to be kept in line as a back bearing. Later, you need to swing out wide to miss a sand bank and head for the fishing quay before turning upstream to the marina on the opposite bank.

The cold channel and the warmth of Concarneau

Actually it was fairly straightforward and, as we soon realised, much simpler than finding a mooring in the marina which was virtually full. The pontoons come out from the bank at right angles and at the end of the middle one was a pontoon parallel with the bank where a British boat was moored. There was a little space in front of her; no more than 20 feet, and to get into it we would have to come into the port side, a manoeuvre *Zefka* does not do well because the propeller pushes her the wrong way.

We decided it was worth getting in there, and that the ebbing current would slow the boat down. The plan was to go in very slowly. Pauline and Jon would need to jump off and hold the boat in while I stopped it by going astern. Fortunately, everything worked pretty well. I managed to miss the bow of the other yacht, but came in close, and stopped it as they hooked some ropes round the cleats. So there we were; relief all round not the least, I imagine, from the couple in the boat behind.

We learned later that they had come across the Channel from the Solent and worked their way down the French coast with quite a few delays. They had been to Audierne before and pointed us at the shops and the supermarket, which is about half a mile up the river. Audierne is a delightful little town, bustling by day and quiet by night.

We were right in the centre of the town, well placed to buy the essential phone cards, and near the market where we had our first experience of buying fruit and vegetables from a French market stall, for many years. The vendor carefully selected the best produce and gave us cherries to sample and a free bunch of parsley. We knew that the French were very particular about the quality of their food and this was evident wherever we shopped in France. The food was relatively inexpensive as well.

There were a few restaurants in the town, but we cooked dinner on the boat. As all three of us are vegetarians, we did not expect to find anything suitable in the town and thought we would fare better in Concarneau. Of course, if you eat meat and fish, you will find a good selection of restaurants near almost all the ports on the route. However, there are fewer restaurants near the marina in Camaret or Concarneau than we had expected.

The Leisurely Route to the Med

We did not really expect to find anyone in the marina office, but the attendant was there although it was quite late. He went out of his way to help us, providing jetons for the showers and toilets which are a few hundred metres from the marina. Before nine o' clock the following morning he left a weather forecast and details of the marks for the channel out to sea.

Sometime during the evening we noticed a couple on our pontoon by the boat, and Pauline said:

'Those people have been there for some time. They must be studying our boat.'

I popped my head out of the main hatch, and saw a middle-aged French couple standing on the pontoon. The man, who we learned later was a veterinary surgeon, started asking questions about junk rig boats, and mine in particular. We invited them aboard, and had a long discussion about the merits of junk rig boats. He said that he currently owned a traditional gaff rigger, but planned to build a 10-metre junk rig yacht to sail off, if not around the world, certainly long distances.

10th June: A leisurely start and a glorious sail down the coast and past the isles of Glénan

That morning we were able to indulge in one of the pleasures of life: buying French bread and bringing it home to eat for breakfast while it is still hot. I remember on an earlier trip to France doing the same thing, and walking back to the boat in company with another yachtie who remarked:

'Amazing isn't it how the French can package air inside a brittle crust and get you to pay money for it?'

I had to agree then that the bread was mostly air, but delicious none the less. It still was. We had a leisurely morning in Audierne because, according to the pilot book, we could not leave until three hours before high water, which would be around midday. Since we had about 40 miles to go to Concarneau, we knew that we would arrive late. We had been to Concarneau by car and thought it looked a pleasant town.

It was almost noon before we did leave and still the water was pretty shallow in the channel, but plenty for us so long as we kept to the markers. There was quite a good breeze out in the bay, and *Zefka* was soon heading south briskly. Before long we could see more magnificent French

The cold channel and the warmth of Concarneau

lighthouses; these two tall towers were the original Eckmuhl lighthouse and its modern replacement off Penmarch Point, where we expected the current to be helping us a little. The wind generally increases around headlands and Penmarch lived up to expectations, but not before the wind had dropped off so that the speed fell back a couple of miles north of the point. As we came to the point, however, the wind increased quite sharply to a good force four, and we were sailing at over six and half knots, and gaining an extra half a knot from the current. We reefed two panels, and continued at a slightly lower speed, soon turning south-east to head around some buoys toward Concarneau.

By the early evening the wind had dropped almost entirely and we were now in a wide bay sheltered from the south west by two groups of islands: Glénan and Moutons. There are a number of bays, inlets and harbours on the north side of the bay, and the islands are beautiful. They were quite low, sandy islets and looked very tranquil sitting there in the calm sea. We wished we had a little more time to explore them—as, indeed, our visitor of the previous evening had recommended—but had to be content with the view and the prospect of Concarneau.

We were still about 12 miles away, and it was easy to appreciate why this is such a popular sailing area, since there are the islands to explore and quite a large expanse of sheltered sea. That evening it was idyllic—except for the lack of wind; the sea was calm, it was warm, the sun was shining and we had almost the whole bay to ourselves.

It is quite difficult to find the buoys that guard the entrance to Concarneau from a distance—the sailor always wants to find these things before he needs them—but once we were near enough to need them they were quite conspicuous. At first, you seem to be entering a river, but soon the marina is evident on the port side in front of the old town. We looked in and went into the first berth that seemed empty.

The moorings were good, but Pauline complains: 'This was our first encounter with narrow, extremely wobbly finger pontoons which resonate uncontrollably and attempt to tip you into the water as you struggle to make fast round a cleat. Once you are moored they seem to calm down and don't pose any problem, but jump down from the boat in a hurry and you could be in trouble!'

The Leisurely Route to the Med

As at Camaret and Audierne, we had to select our own mooring, and we found this was usual practice on the west coast of France, although there are a few exceptions. There were only a couple of conventional cruising yachts in the visitors' berths, the remainder being filled by yachts from the Île de Glénan sailing school, reputed to be the biggest in France. All around were young, athletic looking men—and a few women—either loading their boats or making adjustments very earnestly.

Needless to say the office had closed at 8pm, which meant that the toilets and showers were closed as well. This was pretty well standard for the French marinas in June. Did they expect us to cross our legs from 8pm to 8 or 9am? Of course the French go over the side in full view but we are British! Anyway, this means it is difficult to make use of the facilities if you arrive in the evening and must leave the following morning. What you are paying for then is a sheltered mooring and easy access to the town.

We walked into town to find a restaurant, and although there are quite a few in Concarneau many were closed and most that were open were highly unsuitable for us. In fact, the town looked pretty dead.

'Oh this is hopeless,' said Pauline, 'Let's go back and open a tin or something.'

I persuaded her and Jon to continue a little further and we turned into a narrow side street to see a crêperie that not only looked inviting, but had some suitable fare on the menu. Unlike most of the restaurants we had passed this was almost full; it looked like we had come to the right place.

It was called Le Petit Chaperon Rouge or Little Red Riding Hood. It turned out to be delightful, with nice bright decor inside, and some galettes (savoury crêpes) with mushrooms and spinach. We also wanted salads, but they had been so busy that night that there was just one left for the three of us to share. Actually it was quite large, and delicious, as were the crêpes, which we enjoyed with a bottle of wine. We followed with some crêpes containing fruit, and went back to the boat feeling a good deal better.

The cold channel and the warmth of Concarneau

11th June: A quick recce in Concarneau, followed by another pleasant day as we sailed to Belle Île

We were standing on the boat the following morning when a young woman came up, thrust a card at us and asked how long we were staying. We told her we were leaving that day, and she scribbled something on the card.

'Shall I pay you now?' I asked.

'Non, you pay at the office,' she replied and was gone.

We found the showers and washing facilities were good but quite small, but they enabled Jon to shave for the first time since he left England, so he went off the boat as "Desperate Dan" and returned somewhat transformed. We then had just enough time to stroll into the old fortified town—the Clos Ville—which is full of tourist shops, but nevertheless worth a visit just to see the old streets. It was built initially in the 14th century, and was fortified 200 years later.

Since we had such a long voyage ahead of us, we had decided that the best plan was to hop between some of the islands off the coast of Brittany rather than go along the coast. Jon was limited in the time that he could spend, and we had only seven weeks or so and did not know just how long it would take to reach the Med.

Chapter Three

Belle Île and other islands

BEFORE setting off for Belle Île, which lies outside the Morbihan, a renowned cruising area, we sought out the weather forecast and found that it was on the notice board in the office. The French provide excellent forecasts daily, and on this occasion a northerly force three to four was predicted. There was a little wind to start with, but it soon fell away so we had to motor for most of the day. By 4pm we were off Île de Groix, and had covered 25 miles. The sun continued to shine and there was just a slight swell. The customs officer's claim that the south of Brittany was much warmer than the north was being borne out; it had been appreciably warmer since we turned round Penmarch Point.

By just after six we were approaching Belle Île, and could see that it was well-named. It is like a plateau, about 50 metres high, and the hills roll down into the sea—some say it is similar to the south Cornish coast. There is plenty of greenery on the island, and even some small woods.

The Leisurely Route to the Med

Although there are no marinas, you can moor either in Sauzon or Le Palais, the grand-sounding name of the largest town in the island. Sauzon is a beautiful but short estuary with two pairs of jetties. Boats can anchor outside or moor inside the outer harbour. It looked rather too complicated and narrow, and in any case space is very limited, whereas Le Palais is supposed to have space for 80 boats. So we passed by, although it looked very attractive. According to both the French and British pilot books, there is plenty of room in Le Palais, with mooring buoys and lines on one side and a communal buoy for rafting up on the other. However, as we approached we saw quite a large British yacht come out of the harbour and pick up a buoy nearby. We thought that seemed ominous.

Le Palais is most impressive from the sea. It is heavily fortified on the north side, and there are cliffs to the south, the two breakwaters of the harbour nestling between them—with the usual large lights on each. So in we went; well, there was no buoy on the port side at all, just a small raft which was evidently involved in some repair work. On the other side, there was already a row of boats moored and there appeared to be an empty space right near the entrance, but the owner of the next boat, a Frenchman, shouted out: 'You can't come here.'

Just the sort of bonhomie you want when you arrive in a harbour! We went further, and could see a space at the far end of the pack of yachts, but we could also see that a large car ferry was just going astern off the jetty nearby. It then dropped its two bow anchors and continued to go astern, narrowing the gap between it and the mooring we were considering. We went in a little closer only to be warned off mooring there by the people on that boat, also French, who said they were leaving in the night. I shrugged my shoulders, and did not consider that a problem. But I did consider the fact that the ferry was getting closer and closer a serious problem! So I steered *Zefka* back out into the middle of the harbour while the ferry finished mooring. As we motored past the moored boats a voice said:

'You can come next to us if you like.'

It was a man standing on a large black ketch right in the middle of the harbour, and sure enough there was quite a space next to his boat, Iltis, which was German registered. We duly went alongside, bow in, and the

German couple helped us moor to their buoy. They were most impressed as Pauline used our Swiftie-Matic to get a line through the hoop on the large mooring buoy. It is an amazing device with a rope on a complicated eye on the end of a pole that you just push through the ring on the buoy and pull it back. Hey presto! The rope is attached to the ring, and you just pull it in to secure it.

This very friendly couple were heading for the Mediterranean like us, but were presumably retired, because they said that they were travelling slowly, spending several days wherever they chose, as they did not want to arrive until November.

By the time we had finished mooring, it was a bit late to go ashore—we had covered 48 miles that day after a late start. We looked around. Behind us was a high jetty, and opposite a shingle beach covered in seaweed, where people parked their dinghies. At the far end of the harbour were a number of quaint old buildings including two attractive hotels, one of which was called the Grand Hotel de Bretagne. It all looked very pleasant, and we decided that we would go ashore the following morning.

12th June: Another lovely day with breakfast ashore and some good sailing

The next morning we rowed ashore in the dinghy and sat outside one of the hotels in the sunshine enjoying a breakfast of fresh bread with coffee. From where we sat we could see the ferry come in and the hundreds of people and quite a few cars disembarking. These French ferry crews are just amazing; the ferry seems almost too wide for the harbour entrance when it arrives, but the ship just comes straight in, turns through 90 degrees and moors. That's it. Within a few minutes cars are driving off up the slipway.

It was Saturday, so many people were arriving for the weekend, including a number who were evidently coming home. So the whole area was busy, as people greeted each other, and visitors wondered where to go, and booked bicycles, coaches and cars. It was hustle and bustle all around.

The town has a lively French seaside atmosphere, and is absolutely delightful, with its narrow alleys, several bakers who bake on the premises and, as is the case almost anywhere in France, excellent greengrocers. There are also some banks. We did some necessary shopping, and some that was hardly necessary, such as buying delicious looking pastries in a boulangerie loaded with all sorts of cakes and bread. Cakes and pastries, most bright yellow owing to the large amount of butter in them, seem to be a speciality of the island.

At the back of the harbour we found a lock leading to a narrow river. Many boats were moored in the river where there is also space for visitors. Of course, you need to enter and leave quite near high water. Now we understood why the pilot books indicated that there was space for 80 visiting yachts.

Jon had gone off on his own, and when we returned to the dinghy, he was sitting beside it with a contented smile and a large case of beer. We rowed back to the boat just a little sad that we did not have as much time as the people on the next boat, to explore Belle Île further.

We slipped the mooring just before eleven o' clock, and as we sailed along the coast we were further enchanted by the green hills and sandy beaches to the south. We were heading for another island: Noirmoutier, where there is a marina at L'Herbaudiere, right on the northern tip. The wind started off as a pleasant force three from the north, which enabled us to cruise along gazing delightedly at the island. But within half an hour, the wind had dropped to a force two, so I decided to motor-sail, partly because the batteries seemed a little low. So far we had not bothered to hook up to mains power when we moored because we had not been stopping for long, and of course there was no mains power available on the mooring at Belle Île.

We were pushing against the tide a little; in fact, later on the tide was flowing against us at 1.5 knots according to the GPS. Incidentally, although I was now using the GPS to check our position, I was taking bearings to give a fix of our position where practical. Once we left the southern end of the island, we could see just a little of Hoedic, one of the attractive sandy islands off the Morbihan. After that fell into the distance, we were out of sight of land for some time. Once again the sun shone, and it was a really warm day.

Later in the afternoon, the wind had increased sufficiently to switch off the engine, and *Zefka* gathered pace. With the wind behind, we were soon goose winging along with hardly any load on the tiller, and the speed rising first to just over six knots. As the island came into view, the wind increased and the sea became rougher, but *Zefka* was creaming along at about seven knots, with the speed rising once to over eight knots, and for well over seven knots for much of the time, the speed at which one should be reefing—really exhilarating. However, with not far to go, and the need to turn across the wind to follow the second part of the channel into the marina, we left the full sails up and just kept going.

When the wind increases earlier in the day, we do reef fairly early, not least because when you have 1,500 miles to go it is wise to err on the side of caution. Generally, we were thinking about reefing at six and a half knots, and at a steady seven knots we reef. If the speed gets up to eight knots, when we are running, we've left it too late, and it will take a long time to reef. Of course, because *Zefka* has a large sail area and seven panels, there is still plenty of sail up with a couple of reefs in. Pauline gets somewhat nervous when the speed rises, so the moment when we reef is usually a compromise between our differing views.

On this occasion, by the time the wind was getting strong, we were very close to the approach channel, so it did not seem worth reefing. The first part of the approach channel is marked clearly, but there is quite a current running across the north of the island, so I was steering well off to keep in the channel. Eventually, we lowered the sails, much to Pauline's relief, and motored in through the narrow entrance. Entering a strange marina is usually a little stressful because you do not know whether there will be any room. If there is room, you wonder whether it will be in a reasonable place; whether the water will be deep enough—many are marginal in France—and whether there is a reception pontoon or not. In this case we knew that the visitors' pontoon was on the port; at least, that is what the pilot book told us. It was quite near high water so we knew there should not be any problems with the depth.

As we passed between the two harbour walls, we could see a long pontoon to the port side, and this was obviously the visitors' pontoon. The other pontoons stretched from that into the basin, while the fishing boats were moored on the starboard side. Fortunately, the fairway was nice and wide so we were able to motor up to the end, see what was available, and turn around. There were no empty spaces alongside the pontoon, and already one or two boats were rafted up against others.

I decided to raft up against a French 35-footer with an aluminium hull, since there was plenty of room around, and it was fairly near the entrance. The crew on the French boat consisted of a couple, one child and a toy poodle. They were sitting on the boat, so we indicated that we wanted to come alongside, and the man immediately jumped up and went toward the bow. Meanwhile, the woman, who was dressed rather smartly for sailing, and had long painted nails, stood up in the cockpit. As we drew alongside, almost stationary, but with the tide just moving us out a little, I handed the woman the stern line, and she took it and just stood there. Jon had meanwhile sorted out the bow line with the skipper of the other boat and Pauline was walking back. We both called to the woman to please put the rope around the cleat, but she stood for quite some time before she got the message. By that time, fortunately, the skipper had come aft and quickly tied off the line. Phew!

It was only about seven o' clock as we placed some lines across to the pontoon, and sorted out the springs. Later, the wind dropped, and it was then that we suffered our first assault in foreign waters. Pauline was at the cooker, and Jon and I were in the saloon when I looked through the window and saw a boat moving past very close at what seemed quite a speed. I heard a bit of a noise, and a couple of seconds later it was stationary alongside. Pauline, who had a better view, shot up into the cockpit. She writes:

'I saw this French yacht approaching fast and then it bounced off *Zefka*. I was just in time to receive a line from one of its crew as he leapt aboard our boat and fell sprawling on the deck. I don't recall the engine being put into reverse; they had used Zefka as their brakes.'

Jon and I went on the deck and took the stern line, and initially they put one spring on as well. The comedy was not over. Next, the young man stood on his boat and pulled the ropes in tight—and I mean tight. As he did so a young, obviously pregnant woman, clambered onto *Zefka*, walked along the deck so that she was facing the man and gave him a big kiss. Presumably for his brilliant effort at mooring.

Well, the boat didn't ram us bow on, did it? We studied it later and observed that it was spotlessly clean, without a sign of wear or fading anywhere. Even the ropes were all brand new so this was probably its maiden voyage. If the skipper continued to moor at speed there would soon be signs of wear and tear—and not just on *his* boat!

Later, the wind started to blow much harder and continued to do so for a couple of hours. We were glad to be in the marina. We did not see much of the marina facilities that night, but the following morning we found that the showers were not too bad, and there were a couple of small chandlers, although these were not open because it was a Sunday.

**THE ROUTE:
Plymouth to Bilbao**

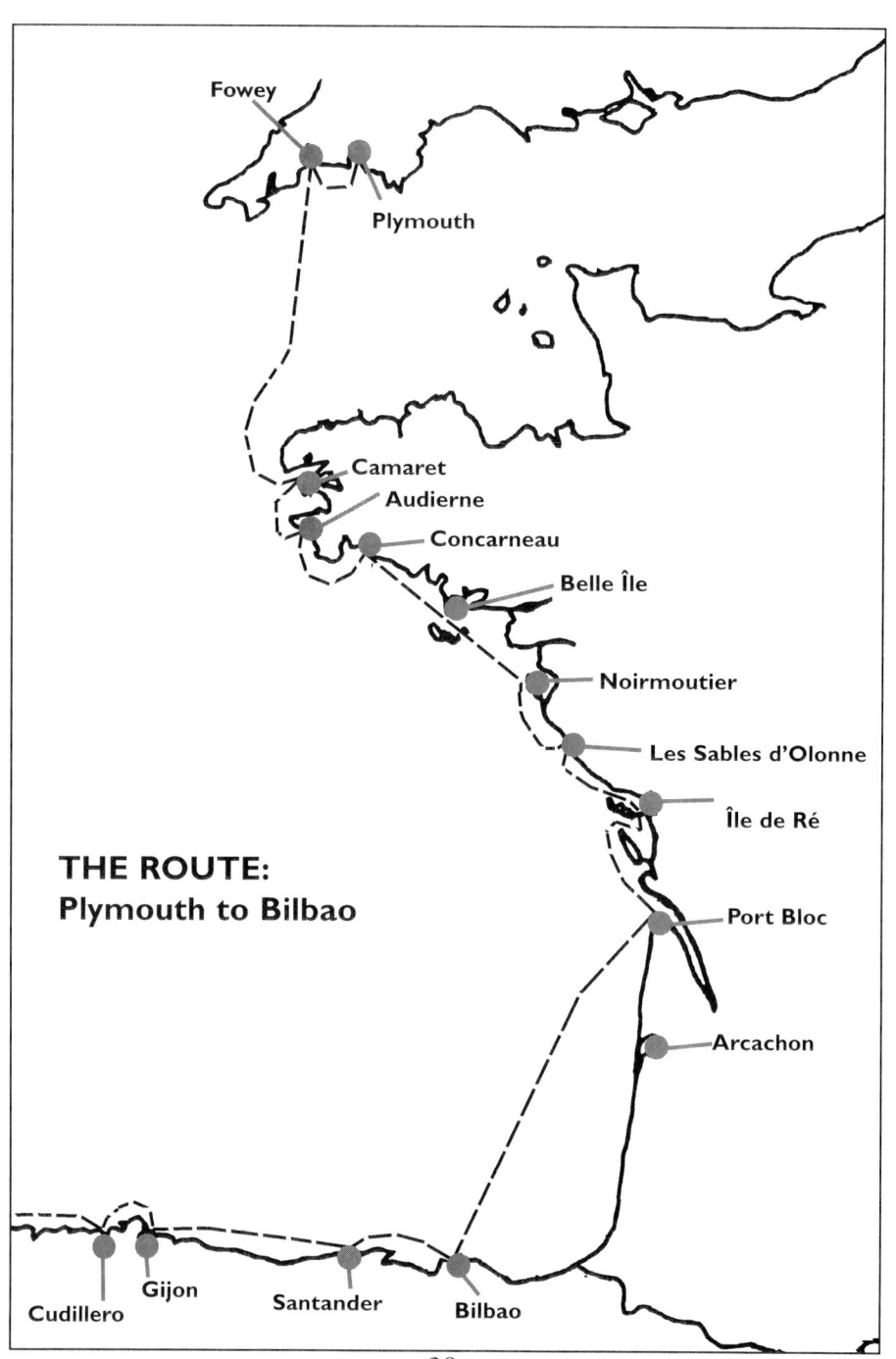

Chapter Four

Good winds to the Île de Ré

13th June: Oops! They may say that you can go out at low tide, but you can't. Exhilarating afternoon made up for the upsetting morning.

WE WERE a bit lackadaisical the next morning, slipping our mooring at low water, but that should not have caused any problems. The information in the British and French pilot books on the dredged depth of the channel into L'Herbaudiere differed, but the actual depth in the channel should have been either 2.1 or 2.3 metres according to which one you believed—either way enough for Zefka which draws 1.6 metres. However, as soon as we moved forward inside the harbour, the depth alarm sounded showing two metres. We headed toward the harbour entrance, thinking that it would be deeper in the middle of the channel.

As we passed between the two breakwaters the view was really spooky; all you could see were reefs towering up behind the little stick that marked the port side of the entrance channel. We went out very slowly, turned sharply into the centre of the channel heading out to sea, and still the

The Leisurely Route to the Med

depth sounder kept screeching, and the depth got less. We could see that there was a sandy bottom, but when the depth gauge was reading 1.2 metres—that is the depth from the sounder on the hull, not the actual depth—I started to get concerned, although we were only moving forward at about one knot. OK, so I should have got concerned a little earlier, but I was simply not expecting that, with all those big fishing boats there, they would not dredge the main channel so near to the harbour.

There was no bump but, about 100 metres from the entrance to the harbour, the sounder reading suddenly dropped to 0.9 metres, and *Zefka* just stopped. We could see the sand being churned up by the propeller, which is well protected by the keel. At first, I thought this was just a little bar, and so went astern and off at an angle; but the same thing happened again. There we were sitting on the sand.

Since it was low water we could have just sat there and waited for the tide, but Jon thought that it would be worth trying to go astern and turn around. We tried it, and *Zefka* went back a few inches, and turned a little. A little more forward, a little more astern, and before long we were broadside on, and could turn off the sand, and head back into the marina. Having given the locals a spot of amusement, we tied up on the first pontoon inside the harbour and went ashore.

The moral of the story, which we found to be the case elsewhere in French marinas, is: don't believe the depths to which they say they are dredged. Instead, give yourself a metre to spare. Also, do not assume, because the pilot book says the port can be entered 24 hours a day, that it can be. L'Herbaudiere cannot. In reality it is available for about four hours each side of high water for a boat with a draft of two metres—and many yachts do have this much draft.

While we were waiting for the tide, we found that the village was quite pleasant, although almost all the buildings were new, no doubt as part of a modern development of the island. There were plenty of tourists, but we relaxed in a little bar over fresh orange juice, bought some postcards and returned to the boat.

We had initially thought of making a fairly short passage to the Île de Yeu, but Jon had called there when sailing from Brittany to the Gironde, and had found it unattractive. Therefore, we had decided, the previous evening, to go as far as Les Sables d'Olonne, a well-known resort. It was about 50 miles away, and so we were once again starting rather late for such a passage. But the important point was that now, at half past twelve, we were able to negotiate the channel from the marina with enough water beneath the keel.

By the time we left the harbour, the wind was fresh so we reefed one panel in each sail and then sailed close to the wind for a mile or so before turning inshore of a small island to run along the coast of Noirmoutier. Noirmoutier is a long, thin island connected to the mainland by a long, arching bridge. The wind was coming from just to the west of north, and the sun still shone, as it did for most of the day, and we made good progress. The warmth in the sun told us that we were definitely going south, and had left Brittany. A favourable wind blew once more, although we did need to shake out the reef after a couple of hours. For most of the time we were running before the wind at around six knots, riding the low swell comfortably.

Gradually, both the wind and swell increased, and *Zefka* surfed over the waves with the sails goose winging. This long distance cruising was easy! By four o'clock, the wind had shifted around to the north, and a little later we overtook another yacht. Otherwise, most of the yachts had been beating north, presumably in a Sunday race. The further south we went, the stronger the wind and *Zefka* raced ahead at over seven knots, gaining another knot over the ground, which helped make up for our late start. By now the swell was quite big, and we decided it was time to reef two panels in each sail.

We were still cracking along as we passed Les Barges lighthouse which we presumed, for some reason, was just short of the entrance to the harbour. In fact, it is on a rock well out to sea and quite a bit to the north of the entrance to Les Sables d'Olonne. About a mile further on we headed toward a pair of buoys that must be passed before entering the harbour, whose entrance resembles a river. Whereas Les Barges lighthouse is a typically magnificent tower, these buoys are quite small and not too easy to distinguish from a distance; in fact, if you are not careful you could imagine that you could turn around the first one and head inwards. But that could be dangerous.

The Leisurely Route to the Med

Zefka was careering on well, but as we were now heading across the large swell the boat was pitching and rolling quite a bit. Eventually, we reached the second buoy, and turned toward the pair of breakwaters that run out to sea. Now, with the wind on the beam we were heeling well over, but the motion was less agitated, because each wave tended to lift us and deposit us gently in the well before the next wave picked us up. Before long, we were close enough to the entrance to lower the sails.

After an exhilarating sail, and one of the best days we were to have, we motored into Les Sables d'Olonne. The two breakwaters are most distinctive; in fact the last 100 metres or so of the northern one is not a breakwater at all, but is more like a bridge with a series of archways beneath. Although the river is quite wide, we noticed that everyone seemed to cling to the south bank so we did likewise. It was quite near low water, and the depth was only about three metres—we were now very wary of shallow water.

On the northern bank is an old and impressive tower and a little further in you pass an inlet on the south side, which leads to the old town and fishing port. There is a speed limit, as in most harbours, and the French word for knots is noeuds. By Les Sables d'Olonne, we were into jokes about how many noeuds—rhyming with the moeths that Peter Sellars talked about when acting as Clouseau—were allowed here or there.

The Port Olona marina is well down the river. We were quite surprised to find a long, empty reception and refuelling pontoon just below the marina office. Even more of a surprise was the fact that after a few minutes the duty officer turned up in a dory, despite it being about 8.30pm. He informed me that the showers and toilets were open from 7am to 10pm. Progress. Then he told me where we would find the berth, and disappeared.

We found C pontoon, but the numbers were difficult to see. We motored forward gingerly, and suddenly Pauline shouted:

'This is 38. Here!'

By now *Zefka's* bow was almost opposite the rather narrow gap, and as I looked around to weigh up the situation so about six heads popped up from boats that, up to that moment, had appeared empty. Of course,

Good winds to the Île de Ré

when you are in this situation they all look disapproving as if to say: 'What a mess he's making and going to make of that.' But in reality they are just curious to see how you handle the boat.

Anyway, with a bit of manoeuvring, *Zefka* went into the narrow gap. Once she settled down the fenders remained in contact with both the pontoon and adjacent boat. All the other boats on that pontoon seemed to be 29-30 feet long, so it was a tight squeeze.

The finger pontoons were once again short and very bouncy, which did not do much for Pauline's sense of security as she tied on the first ropes. By the time she had leapt onto the pontoon, all those heads had disappeared again. It was very still in the yacht basin, although the wind was still blowing, and we unwound after a good but long day, in which we had covered 48 miles, all under sail, and had averaged six knots. It was an excellent marina, but you do need to watch the depth. It went down to about 2.5 metres in the berth and some of the fairway.

After dinner we went out for a walk, and found that the marina is part of a new development of flats, which are quite tasteful, and there are a couple of restaurants, and also a baker nearby. Nearer the sea is part of the old town with narrow streets running between small and attractive houses.

14th June: A short and pleasant run to the beautiful Île de Ré

In the morning we tested the showers and found them quite good. However, not only were there no toilet seats—not uncommon in France—but unusually, there were not even fixing holes for seats! The French have definitely got a thing about toilet seats, we decided, but they've come a long way from their holes in the ground.

We left at about ten o'clock, refuelling on the way out. We had the choice of going on to La Rochelle or Île de Ré, but not really time to visit both. Owing to the state of the tide, we would not be able to go right into the marina in the town at La Rochelle, and Jon had found Île de Ré a lovely place. We had seen an aerial photograph of the harbour which is surrounded by the old fortified town, and so were eager to go there anyway. Saint Martin, Île de Ré just had to be the choice. There is a lock at the entrance to the marina so we timed our departure to arrive at Saint Martin about two hours before high water when the lock would have opened a half an hour or so earlier.

Once again the sun shone, and as we hoisted the sails in the large sandy bay that gives Les Sables d'Olonne its name, it was very hot with just a gentle breeze coming from the north. It was enough to allow us to sail for an hour, but then dropped off so we had to motor-sail. Gradually the wind increased and by early afternoon we were just off the northern point of Île de Ré, with the wind a pleasant force three or four. Generally, we had found that the wind would remain steady during the afternoon increasing at about five o' clock, but on this occasion the wind decided to come early, so soon we were hustling along at around seven knots.

After rounding the first cardinal buoy to head toward the harbour entrance, we had the wind on the beam, and *Zefka* shot forward. Even when we let the sails out to spill the wind still the boat powered forward, heeling quite a lot. We were all sitting on the coaming well above the sea with *Zefka* racing along when a 40-foot yacht, which had just come out of the port, turned to the south and started to motor off. The crew looked at *Zefka,* and then continued looking; they seemed spellbound by this strange craft—there are very few junk rig boats in France—so that when we waved nonchalantly they did not notice at first. Eventually, they waved back, and continued to stare until we had passed.

After that bit of fun, we took the sails down and started to concentrate on entering Port St Martin. We could see the church on the hill behind the harbour, but the entrance is hidden behind a seawall which is actually an island clad in wooden pilings. This breakwater is shaped like a chevron. Behind it is the channel which takes you into the harbour where it divides into two forks; small local boats turn left, others turn right to the marina. Alongside the first part of the channel is a waiting pontoon on one side, and old buildings on the other. The channels throughout the port run between old harbour walls of light yellow sandstone.

It was when we had passed the pontoon and came to a fork in the channel that the scene just took our breath away. Straight ahead, many little boats were moored alongside the harbour walls, and the water was surrounded by beautiful old buildings, either sandstone or painted. The harbour actually resembles canals threading their way through the town.

Good winds to the Île de Ré

Then, we looked to the right-hand fork, and could see what looked like a French country scene. There was the old lock, open to receive us, and to one side the traditional building that served as the office for the marina, with trees and grass behind. On the left-hand side were beautiful flowering shrubs in front of an old building. What a memorable scene!

In fact, the canals have been dug out to completely surround an almost rectangular island, which is joined to the mainland by a breakwater. Therefore, in one side of the harbour, the lock is used to maintain a suitable water level, and the other side the harbour dries out.

I quickly concentrated again, and saw that the harbour master was standing on the quay and shouting out to ask how long we were staying. I had already grandly said that the crew could have 24 hours shore leave here, and when we told him 'two days' he told us to raft up 'au bord du vedette', pointing to a 40-foot motor cruiser which appeared to be a permanent resident. We turned in, and there we were alongside. Although it was still the middle of June, there were only a handful of spaces in the marina, so in August, it must be difficult to find a berth there.

It was now over a week since we had left Plymouth. Some of that time had been interesting, some exhilarating, some uncomfortable and some relaxing. But there had never been any question about what we needed to do. Each day we had to sail to cover the miles. Now, we felt the need for a day off, and what better place to take it than St Martin, Île de Ré?

We had about the best place in the marina because we were near one end, and since there was a slipway ahead of us there was not room for a boat to raft up against *Zefka*. Not too much later a British-registered Moody 34 came in and motored a short distance up the harbour before wriggling into a space next to one yacht but with two behind and two in front. We saw that Plymouth was shown as the home port on the stern. Later the owner, seeing that our boat was also from Plymouth came over to have a chat. He actually kept his boat at Rochefort, which is just south of La Rochelle, and was spending most of his time in France.

During the conversation we discussed our plans for the voyage across the Bay of Biscay. He told us that the main problem was that there was a large area north of Arcachon which the French military uses for firing exercises and that it extends about 45 miles out to sea. He advised going directly to the Spanish coast to avoid it, whereas we had been planning to go to Arcachon.

Evidently a friend of his had been sailing to Arcachon about ten miles off the coast, when a helicopter had suddenly appeared. One of the crew leaned out of the cockpit waving a board with a number on it. The sailor did not know it meant 'Tune your VHF to this channel,' so he ignored it. About 15 minutes later a French military ship came alongside and escorted him out of the no-go area. This information gave us something to think about.

But first to St Martin: we explored the area around the port, and were not disappointed. It really is a lovely town, with just a few small hotels and many restaurants around the harbour. We found a restaurant overlooking the harbour where we could sit sipping coffee as we enjoyed the atmosphere. It is marvellous after you have been sailing for a day or even a few hours, hardly seeing another boat, to come into a popular tourist resort, sit down and enjoy the activity.

Afterwards, we strolled along a narrow alley that ran up the slope from the harbour inland; there were a few shops, including one specialising in good wines, and an attractive food shop. Most of the houses are old and all are tastefully built. That evening we were going to eat out, come what may, and after looking at the menu in almost every restaurant decided that Marco Polo, an Italian restaurant, offered the best choice for us. We stopped at a Spanish-style bar for drinks and two large bowls of guacamole with nachos, before moving on to Marco Polo.

The next day was warm and sunny. We were looking forward to a walk along the coast path, but first, there were the inevitable chores—a day off on a voyage of this type is not really a day off. It wasn't too bad, though, because there was a decent washing machine at the marina, and shopping in France is always fun. By the time we set out for our walk—Jon had gone off elsewhere—*Zefka* was bedecked with washing on every inch of guardrail, on the booms, the sprayhood and some extra lines we had rigged up. The sun was hot, the place was beautiful, and the washing would be dry in a couple of hours. The rain and cold of Plymouth and Fowey seemed a million miles away; we had actually covered 370 nautical miles.

We did have plenty of time for a walk so we set off along the coast path to La Flotte, a small seaside town. After leaving St Martin we came to the Citadel, which was presumably part of the fortified defences in Napoleonic times. It has its own tiny harbour, which is now silted up with sand leaving it high and dry at low water. The harbour has high walls all around, and to enter you would need to take a dog leg course; it is probably big enough for a 30-footer or so.

From the citadel, the path to La Flotte is mostly along a low cliff just above the beach. Apart from the odd cove, the beach is of indifferent quality and spoiled by the hundreds of artificial beds for farming shellfish. These were exposed by the low tide, and seeing so many all together certainly opens your eyes. Such vast numbers of shellfish growing in such a small space must have an adverse effect on the ecology of the island. Of course, as with most such changes brought about by man, it will be years, if not decades, before the full effects are seen.

La Flotte is a pretty little town. It has a small harbour, which can be entered only near high water owing to the sand banks outside, and there doesn't appear to be any space for visitors; if there is, it will be for boats of up to about 25 feet. Nevertheless, it is a nice place to sit out in the open at one of the restaurants. We chose La Fiancée du Pirate, a crêperie, for lunch and enjoyed savoury wholemeal crêpes with mushrooms and a salad as we watched the world go by.

They mostly seem to go by in La Flotte on bicycles. First came an upright model, with capacious basket in front, ridden sedately by a genteel old lady who stopped to buy provisions before returning home with long baguettes protruding from her basket. A very weathered old man pedalled slowly past, a retired fisherman or farmer perhaps? Then suddenly the harbour road was alive with bicycles as a long procession of children passed by on modern bikes of varying sizes, preceded by an athletic-looking man, presumably their teacher. These were the keen ones. There was a long gap before the last stragglers pedalled wearily past with good-natured encouragement from their escort at the rear. Very few cars marred the peace of that lunch. The idyllic atmosphere continued as we walked back beneath a deep blue sky on that warm summer's afternoon.

The Leisurely Route to the Med

Back in the town we went in search of a drill bit I needed to mount a warning lamp that replaced the broken original. The first ironmonger we visited, about 100 metres from the harbour, could not help but the assistant directed us to another one. We walked up the alley to another street and right near the end we came to a truly amazing place, a real old-fashioned ironmonger.

Even in the windows there was a varied assortment of items, and when we walked in and stood on the bare boards of the floor, we felt we were in another age. We could see a fat, elderly man sitting at an ancient desk just inside the doorway with a woman, presumably his wife, standing beside him. The other side of the desk was a middle-aged man who appeared to be just passing the time of day.

The man behind the desk asked what we wanted, and I explained in my indifferent French. He appeared to understand and sent his wife to serve us. She went to the other side of the shop, and started hunting among the tiny drawers behind the counter. We looked around; the place was packed with goods, including a big selection of tools, some agricultural implements, cooking utensils, and all the other things you used to find in ironmongers.

The woman managed to find some drills but not the sort we were looking for, so eventually her husband came over to assist and hunted through more drawers without success. We did buy a couple of things there, though, and we could see that our visit and my poor French made their day; it made ours too.

Just beyond the shop and off the street was an ornate archway which had been the old entrance to the town in the days when it was completely fortified. Beyond the archway was a bridge across what would have been a moat, now just a grassy trench. One more fascinating aspect of St Martin.

Chapter Five

Now for the south Bay of Biscay

16th June: An early start, with the wind coming up in the afternoon to take us to the mouth of the Gironde

WITH A long passage ahead of us, and the need to catch the current between the south of the Île de Ré and the mainland, we slipped the mooring at 6.40am. It was a beautiful clear morning, and the sun was just rising as we raised the sails. Already, a slight breeze blew from the northwest, but not enough so we motor-sailed. We wanted to make sure that we arrived at the south of the island in time for the southerly current to take us through the narrow channel between the island and the mainland. Within a few minutes we met a large black ketch motor-sailing north, but otherwise the sea was deserted; not even a fishing vessel out there.

From Île de Ré we could either sail to the Île d'Oleron, which was not very far, or go straight down to the mouth of the Gironde—Royan is the biggest port in the area. We decided to head straight to Royan which involves a passage of about 60 miles. Île de Ré is about five miles off the land, and we motor-sailed midway between the flat island and unremarkable coast of the mainland for about an hour. Then, we were approaching the narrow channel to the south of the island and the bridge that connects it to the mainland. Here, the channel is only about a quarter of a mile wide, so the tide flows quite fast.

We passed under the high, arching bridge just after eight o' clock. Just to the south of the bridge on the mainland is the large commercial port that serves La Rochelle. There were several ships, one or two standing by, and some small boats in the area.

By the time we turned west to pass the north of the Île d'Oleron, the wind had disappeared altogether. The sea was like the proverbial millpond on a settled summer's day, and the sails just hung there, idle. Apart from the drone of the engine, all was still and quiet. A faint haze hung over the water, reducing visibility, and the sea was uncannily smooth. *Zefka's* bow cut through the water making ripples which fanned out leaving a long trail behind. Could this idle stretch of water really be part of the infamous Bay of Biscay? We passed the island, which like the Île de Ré is connected to the mainland by a bridge at its south, and gradually the wind increased. By lunchtime we were able to switch off the engine, which as always was a big relief, and we continued to make good progress.

By three o' clock we were entering the main shipping channel into the Gironde, which actually starts a few miles out to sea. From here large ships are obliged to call up the Bordeaux control tower to ascertain whether they may enter the river or not. It was only a couple of hours after low water, so few large ships were entering or leaving. We set *Zefka* up to goose wing our way into the Gironde, since the wind had gone round slightly to the west, and off we went, with the current giving us an extra three or four knots.

We were just into the Gironde, and opposite a beach when an inflatable launch came from the coast heading straight at us very fast. We thought it unlikely to be official because it carried a large flag on a short mast, but were intrigued. There were three people on board, and the flag proclaimed that the boat was from a sailing school. They raced up to us, went around the bow at a reasonable distance, turned to drive round

Zefka, studying the sails, and then disappeared back to the coast as fast as they had come. Just curious.

Initially, we had planned to stay in the marina at Royan, but previously Jon had found the staff unhelpful and the port very dirty, so he was keen to go elsewhere. It is a busy port, not just for yachts cruising down the coast, but also for those entering the Gironde to take the canal route to the Mediterranean, as Jon had done. I had mentioned that there was a small marina opposite Royan and now Jon was studying the pilot book to find it.

'Ah, I remember it now,' he said, 'Port Bloc. It is quite a small marina, but looks much nicer and cleaner than Royan. Why don't we go there? It will save us about five miles today and another five tomorrow.'

'Does the pilot book mention any problems?' I asked. We both poured over it, and saw that the main problem was the current; it would be about half tide when we would turn inshore, so it would be running at its fastest, but we were both used to such cross-currents from our sailing around Guernsey.

'It won't be too far before we get behind the jetty on that headland so I think it's worth doing,' I said.

'What about the shopping we need?' asked Pauline.

'Well, there is a ferry across to Royan so we could go over tomorrow morning,' I replied. She did not sound too convinced, but we decided on Port Bloc.

When we were nearing the headland before Port Bloc we lowered the sails and moved over to the south side of the wide river. Soon we could see that the harbour was in a little bay. Although the sea was very confused, as soon as we turned around the marker buoy, *Zefka* held her line easily through the current, and we motored straight in through the wide entrance between substantial breakwaters.

Once inside, we were in a wide basin with some commercial ships on the outer breakwater, and a row of small boats moored at pontoons on the other side. There was no one around, so after making a small circuit we went into the first gap we could find. After we had moored alongside the finger pontoon, an elderly man wandering down the pontoon stopped to look at us. I asked if we were all right there.

'For how long?' he asked in French.

I told him that we were staying just one night.

'In that case no problem,' he replied, 'Although there is less swell at the far end.'

We had not noticed any swell whatsoever in the harbour, and so were a little surprised. When I asked where the toilets and showers were he pointed to a small yellow block and said that the toilets were there.

'But this is just a small marina, privately owned. It is run by the people who keep their boats here so we have no showers,' he said.

A little later on another elderly man came and collected the money and told us that we would find the weather forecast on a building at the far end of the harbour. He also seemed to be retired, and the next day we saw about half a dozen evidently retired men moving an old raft with the aid of the mobile crane. It looked like a well-run marina, although the toilets were of the old fashioned French type with pissoir out in the open and pretty awful. Basically, it is a good haven—although a little shallow below the pontoons at low water—but lacks the facilities of the large, modern marina.

Port Bloc's main role seems to be as the ferry port for cars crossing the Gironde, largely because there are a number of resorts south of Port Bloc. They use some rather strange car ferries which have decks sloping fore-and-aft. The angle of these decks match those of the slipway precisely so that whatever the state of the tide the angle of the two surfaces is always the same, so cars can drive on and off directly. Strange but neat.

At low water we found that there was less than 1.5 metres of water, and *Zefka* sunk into the mud. Not by very much, but she definitely could not be rocked. According to the pilot book, the minimum depth was three metres!

That night we discussed where we were to go next. We had checked with the navigational warnings we had been sent over the Navtex receiver and these confirmed that the area used for firing exercises stretched from three miles off the coast to 45 miles out. It would not be safe to keep

Now for the south Bay of Biscay

within the three-mile limit because that would put us on a lee shore, and it is not practical to go through the sandbanks into Arcachon in bad weather. The next port, Capbreton is not easy either because there is a long narrow channel pointing straight out to sea. Large rollers can form in the channel, so there is the danger of grounding in the troughs of the waves.

Jon had suggested that we went to Arcachon overnight, and then proceed from Arcachon to Bilbao or Capbreton. However, if we were to go from Arcachon to Bilbao directly, we would need another night at sea. Because Jon wanted to travel back to the UK by train, we had decided to go to Bilbao rather than Santander as it is nearer the French border. It also has a much easier entrance than Santander, which could be useful if we were caught by some rough weather—after all, we were heading across the south corner of the Bay of Biscay.

Almost together Jon and I realised that we might as well go directly from Port Bloc to Bilbao, which would involve two nights at sea. That would enable us to cross part of the off-limits zone at night. Incidentally, the situation would be different in July and August when there is no firing—but it would be worth checking that this is the case. We decided to go the next evening, because the weather forecast was quite good, and we should get beyond the firing area by early the morning after.

17th June: Nice breakfast, long walk to the shops, and quizzed by customs on the way out.

The next morning we had breakfast in the one restaurant that was open, and very good it was too; we also used their toilets, which were excellent. Instead of bothering with the ferry to Royan, we decided to walk into the nearest village, Verdon, for some shopping. According to one of the men in the marina, the village was only about one kilometre away—or at least, that was what my ears heard— but soon after we set out we saw a sign indicating that it was four kilometres! We were not dismayed because it was a fine sunny day. Also, we passed some bus stops so we thought we could get a bus back.

Eventually we arrived at the village to discover that the supermarket was still another six kilometres away! Undeterred, we bought essential provisions in the small general store and some bread and tarts in the baker's. We asked about buses to Port Bloc in both shops and they were very positive about a service but indicated different places for the bus stop. Were these people just trying not to disappoint us? We don't know but, while drinking coffee in a bar, we asked again about the bus.

'There is no bus to Port Bloc,' the barman told us.

'Where can we get a taxi?' we asked all innocently.

'You won't find one here,' came the reply.

Crestfallen, we asked the shortest way back to Port Bloc and set off. The sun was hot, the shopping quite heavy, and we hoped this route would be shorter than the way we had come. When we were still in the village, a car pulled up opposite, the door opened, and the driver beckoned to us to get in. It was an old Ford Fiesta, and he took us quickly to Port Bloc—right to the marina. We thanked him profusely.

We wondered where our driver came from. Was he in the bar? Or did the owner of one of the shops, where we had been, ask him to give us a lift? Of course, we never found out, but were grateful to the villager or villagers of Verdon for their kindness.

Before long we came across a minor calamity. While stowing the shopping *someone* had put the box of cakes on the top step of the companionway and *someone else* had stood on it—no one seemed to admit to these acts! Anyway, we can confirm that tartes aux pommes are delicious even when squashed quite badly.

We had a snooze after lunch in preparation for the long passage to Bilbao and later Jon went to have a look at the beach while I planned the route. According to the man who seemed to run the marina, it was best to leave Port Bloc at high water, although no information on tidal streams is available south of the Gironde. Therefore, after dinner, we left the pontoon at about half past eight, which gave us 11 hours in which to cut the corner off the no-go zone before they started firing at 7.30am. We should arrive at the extremity of the area, 45 miles offshore by then, and once we were that far out, we would be able to turn almost due south to Bilbao. The course would be a bit of a dogleg of about 170 miles, and it was likely to take about 33 hours.

Now for the south Bay of Biscay

We were all slightly apprehensive about heading out across the Bay of Biscay even if it was just across the corner. After all, we had intended to keep to the coast but now it seemed we were planning to cross quite a big chunk of the Bay. This was the biggest challenge of the voyage so far. I had heard so many horror stories about the Bay of Biscay, and how the weather could change quickly, and with two nights at sea there was plenty of opportunity for a change in the weather. Nor are there any practical ports of refuge. If the weather turned bad we would have to turn out to sea to get as much sea room as we could, and avoid being swept towards the lee shore. However the weather forecast indicated that we should have no problems for the first 24 hours. After that, even if the weather turned nasty we should be able to make Bilbao, which can be entered in any weather safely.

Of course, having been unexpectedly seasick in the Channel, the thought crossed my mind that I needed to be careful not to let that happen again. So, as we slipped our mooring, we were a bit apprehensive for various reasons.

As soon as were clear of the little bay, the river was like a cauldron and the waves were higher than when we arrived. We went straight out to the buoy, but noticed that one of the pilot boats that came out after us cut the corner; but if he did not know where the channels were, who would?

There was quite a swell running that night and the wind was fresh so we waited until we were in the mouth of the river before raising the sails. As we were doing so, Pauline said:

'There's a grey ship very close. He seems to be following us. I think it's the customs.'

I looked round and could see the vessel, a grey launch of about 50 feet, but ignored it as I hauled up the sail—since the wind was fresh we were starting off with one panel reefed in each sail. By the time I had finished, the customs launch was very close and just behind *Zefka*. Suddenly we heard from a loudspeaker:

'Yacht *Zefka* we are calling you. Channel ten please.'

Sighing, but at least grateful that they had waited until we had raised the sails, I went down and called them up. They asked where we were going. I suppose boats that leave just before dark are likely to attract their attention. Anyway, I told him as patiently as I could that we were heading for Bilbao and that we had been through customs formalities at Camaret. He thanked me and wished us a good voyage. Mind you there was a bit of muttering on *Zefka* about how the customs like to put the frighteners on yachties—and it certainly is disconcerting to be hailed in that way as you are just leaving on a testing passage.

By the time this little interlude was over it was after nine when we headed off on a south-westerly course to clear a series of marker buoys off the coast. It was still quite light, and we were able to see good beaches and a couple of resorts on the coast. We were actually passing between the coast and a big sandbank, which we could just see, despite the beacon not being lit until it was virtually dark, which we found surprising. The wind was coming from the north-west and started at about a force four, but increased somewhat after dark, as did the swell. As midnight approached the wind freshened further so we reefed the second panel. In fact, the wind was to remain steady throughout the night and next day, and we made good progress, initially on a beam reach, but later with the wind from a little further behind.

During the night we operated a watch system in which two people were on and one resting, because I felt that this was better than one on and two off in the Bay of Biscay at night. We had started with the same system across the channel but it had not really worked. This time we were all well and able to keep to the rota, but since it meant we all had little sleep, we continued the system throughout the day.

Perhaps because we are not hardened long-distance cruisers, we are very safety conscious, particularly at night, when we always wear life jackets with lifelines clipped on, both in the cockpit and on deck. It is almost impossible to find someone who falls overboard at night, as the deaths of a number of experienced sailors, some on short passages, show. Also, we make it a rule that if someone needs to go out of the cockpit, he or she is clipped on, and there must be someone left in the cockpit— not snoozing below. It is so easy to slip and fall. We were confident that *Zefka* could handle any weather, it was our job to make sure we stayed with her.

Now for the south Bay of Biscay

The night passed uneventfully, *Zefka* sailing comfortably over the swell. We had seen a yacht sailing north just before 10pm, but after that we had not seen a vessel of any sort for hours, until at around 4am when Pauline and Jon were on watch, they saw lots of lights ahead.

Jon exclaimed:

'This is ridiculous. Nothing for hours. Now look: Spaghetti junction!'

They could see a cluster of lights that turned out to be no less than five ships. Two were moving slowly to starboard, the third went off to port while the other two remained stubbornly off the port bow on a constant heading—that meant we were on a potential collision course. In fact, as *Zefka* drew closer, Pauline and Jon could see bright lights on the two boats which showed they were pair fishing, and it became apparent that they were stationary. Zefka cruised past without altering course. We did not see another boat until we were close to the Spanish coast.

18th June: A superb day's sailing across the Bay of Biscay, crowned by a visit from dolphins!

By 6am we had covered 50 miles, and were still crossing the corner of the firing exercise area. I had cut in a bit closer than when we planned initially on the basis that they would not start firing at exactly 7.30am, and would not be aiming right at the periphery of the area anyway! In fact, it was at about eight o' clock when we emerged into 'safe' water, and by then the swell had increased. We did not hear any firing at all that day.

None of us had any difficulty in keeping awake during the first night, or early in the morning. At sunrise, I felt fine, but a little anxious when I saw the sky which looked ominous. The sun was visible through pinkish cloud, surrounded by a halo, a sight I had seen often in Devon just before bad weather. We still had a long way to go, and had not had a weather forecast for 24 hours. I did not mention it to anyone, but every ten minutes or so I would look up at the sky on the horizon to see if it changed. Gradually, the pink gave way to a brighter, yellow sky and then the sun came up over the cloud. Half an hour later, the sun was shining brightly through a blue sky so I relaxed. That blue sky was to remain with us all day.

The Leisurely Route to the Med

One of the amazing things about the Bay of Biscay is its depth. It suddenly goes from under 100 metres near the coast to great depths of over 1,000 metres in a short distance, and this rapid change in depth is one reason why it gets so rough. There is also a gully running from just off the Gironde towards Bilbao, so by the time we had covered 50 miles we were in over 500 metres of water, and for much of the passage the depth was over 1,000 metres. We knew this not from our depth sounder, but from the charts, because the depth sounder seemed to freak out when the depth reached over 100 metres and would think that the actual depth was only 9 metres or 1.5 metres or something equally ridiculous. Disconcerting at first, but of course the GPS convinced us that the depth sounder had temporarily gone bonkers. Ah, the joys of electronics.

We all reached our nadir of wakefulness at some time or other. Mine came between 10 and 11am that morning, so when I was off watch I slept, which revived me. That seemed to be the key; when you are off watch in the day, get some sleep. Jon seemed to be worst in the afternoon, and Pauline suffered most during the second night.

Jon seemed to be able to sit below reading without ill effects even when the boat was rolling quite considerably. We lesser mortals had to be content with looking at the view, mostly endless sea and sky, so Pauline thought she would be very bored. She says:

'In the past, I have travelled very long distances by car and motor caravan on the Continent, often overnight. When driving it is vital to stay 100% alert and even in the passenger seat your senses are bombarded continuously by the sight and sounds of the traffic, the rapidly passing scenery, and the endless music from the tape player, which seems necessary when travelling this way. You must remain strapped to your seat for hours on end interspersed with occasional stops at busy motorway service areas.'

'But in a boat, with a vacant sea and sky, the hours slip past unnoticed. Of course, you must keep watch, but in reasonable weather during the day this is an intermittent task, usually without any urgency. You can sleep in comfort, cook meals and eat them, and even attend to calls of nature without upsetting the peace. Sure, you get tired when sailing through the night, but not bored as I thought I would.'

Now for the south Bay of Biscay

Even so, on a passage that is longer than your norm, you do find yourself wondering how much further there is to go, especially in the early stages. Gradually we stopped doing this, and just enjoyed the sunshine, the company, the favourable wind and concentrated on whatever we were doing at that moment.

However, there are important points to be noted in any voyage; our next was at about midday when we were exactly due west of Cap Ferrat—50 miles out to sea, giving us plenty of searoom. During the afternoon we ran the engine for about an hour and a half to charge the batteries and make sure that we had sufficient power to see us through the night. We did this because the pair of domestic batteries did not seem to hold their charge as long as they should. We later found that during the refit, the battery switch had been incorrectly labelled, so we were actually draining the smaller starting battery, and not the domestic batteries at all!

The day continued fine and sunny, and reasonably warm, but not so that we could start stripping sweaters off. Throughout the day, the swell kept the boat corkscrewing, but the motion was not as bad as in the Channel, and we continued to cruise along, at over six knots nearly all the time. That evening, Pauline cooked an excellent dinner which we all enjoyed. Actually, this represented progress in her sea legs as she says:

'In the past, I had been able to prepare food below only in a flat calm. Now I discovered that my body had adjusted to the perpetual motion of the boat so that I could work below while the boat pitched and rolled without even feeling queasy. When you reach this stage the still land can become uncomfortable instead. You can be sitting in a bar or having a shower when you realise that the solid world is rocking gently!'

Our dinner consisted of a nut roast—a rehydrated meal—jacket potatoes and a tin of peas bought in France with some gravy. It was all delicious, and we wondered just how it is that the French can produce tinned peas that are so tasty whereas the ones you buy in the UK are so awful. Something to do with the fact that the French really care about their food, and won't buy it unless it is good.

We had a surprise visit that evening—some dolphins came toward the boat. We had seen two or three a couple of times previously on the voyage but this time about ten came, swimming along both sides, then diving beneath the boat to leap out alongside. Then they would disappear astern only to reappear, jumping out of the water as they played with *Zefka*. We watched entranced. Every time we have seen dolphins near the boat we have felt uplifted. They really seem such joyful creatures.

We were making rather better progress than expected, and by 9.15pm had covered 136 miles, leaving about 35 miles to go to Bilbao, or rather, the port of Bilbao since the city itself is about 10 miles inland. By about half past ten, we could make out the contours of the mountains behind the coast of northern Spain, and the light from the nearest lighthouse was visible about an hour later. This sight, and the consequence that we were nearing our destination cheered everyone up, although Pauline was feeling extremely sleepy. She was reluctant to drink any coffee when she was on watch in case it stopped her sleeping later on.

By midnight, the wind had dropped considerably and we were moving toward the land at less than five knots, but were now only 15 miles or so from the breakwater. We could distinguish several lights, and as usual the trick was to decide which were lighthouses, which were ships, and which were city lights. On this passage, the lighthouses were fairly easy to spot since they are high up, although I did hear Jon and Pauline having a difference of opinion about whether one light was actually a lighthouse while I was below.

By about 2am, the long, high waves of the swell had diminished, so the sea seemed almost flat to us. An hour later, and after sailing across 165 miles in 30 hours, we entered between the two breakwaters at the port of Bilbao. It was a great moment, although we did not realise we had more than four miles more to go to our final destination! The entrance to the port is very strange. There is a long breakwater leading from the land to the west of the port right to the entrance, and then there is a short breakwater, just a concrete island about 100 metres long to the east of the entrance. According to the charts, they had planned to extend that breakwater right to the bottom of the cliff to the east of Bilbao several years ago, but nothing has been done. There are some quite dangerous rocks just beneath the cliff, so if one is coast hopping from the east in the dark great care is needed. Even though we were coming from the northeast we had to keep making sure that we were far enough to the west of the cliff; there is a natural tendency to cut corners.

Now for the south Bay of Biscay

Once we had passed the breakwater, we turned south-east as advised in the Seafile, and were surprised to find another set of breakwaters about two miles later. This was the entrance to the commercial port itself. At this point I decided to radio ahead to the marina at Getxo, and was agreeably surprised—no, stunned would be more accurate—to get a response indicating that we could go straight in. A little later we passed the control tower for the port.

Getxo marina is one of the newest in northern Spain, and is easier to find and enter than the old marina, where there is evidently not much room for visitors. We found the entrance easily enough and as we turned around it, wondering where on earth we should go, we saw a lamp waving on a pontoon. The night guard was there to meet us, and showed us to an empty pontoon—there were plenty—and helped us moor. Afterwards he gave us a key for the gate to the pontoon, a card for entry to the shower/toilet block, and a short lead to connect from their 32Amp sockets to our 16Amp lead! Were we impressed! It was 4.05am, four or five hours earlier than I had expected us to arrive, so we had had a very satisfactory sail.

Pauline went up to the toilets, which were open, and reported that a crowd of people were still living it up in one of the bars by the marina. It was a Friday night, but that told us we had arrived in Spain! Evidently, the jetty beside the marina, where there are a dozen or so bars and restaurants, is THE place for Bilbao people to visit at the weekend. It was packed with cars and people most of the time we were there.

Getxo marina is excellent in every way. The pontoons are good, as are the toilets, showers and washing machines, with good security. However, the marina is very expensive; indeed at £18 a night 50% more than any other marina we stayed in on the voyage.

Needless to say, we slept late the following morning, and after trying to find some breakfast in a bar—and failing, which is unusual in Spain—we went to the office while Jon packed up. He had come to the end of the time he could spare, and was returning to England. After we had completed the formalities in the office, we asked the marina manager about the tidal flow since none were shown in the Seafile.

The Leisurely Route to the Med

'Ah,' he said, 'We don't really have any information. There are no diamonds like you have on your charts. The sea goes up and the sea goes down. No charts to show which way it goes.'

He had obviously been asked the same question by many British crews. In fact, as we were to learn, there are appreciable currents flowing along the north and west coast of Spain, but at less than one and a half knots. Around the British coast, tidal currents of this strength are documented because they are considered significant, and they most certainly are for small boats, especially in heavy weather. Whether the Spaniards don't think they matter, or whether they could never be bothered to find out I don't know, but you can be sure that the fishermen know all about them.

Jon had found out how to get to the station, and was ready to set off. We were really sorry to see him go, having enjoyed his company and skills for the previous fortnight or so, but at the same time we were looking forward to continuing our adventure on our own. It turned out that Jon had to take a train to the border and then get the TGV to Paris and another train to Calais. He lives in Kent, and arrived home 24 hours later, which is a great deal quicker than it would have been by ferry—even if the ferry had gone that day instead of two days later.

**THE ROUTE:
Bilbao to Minho**

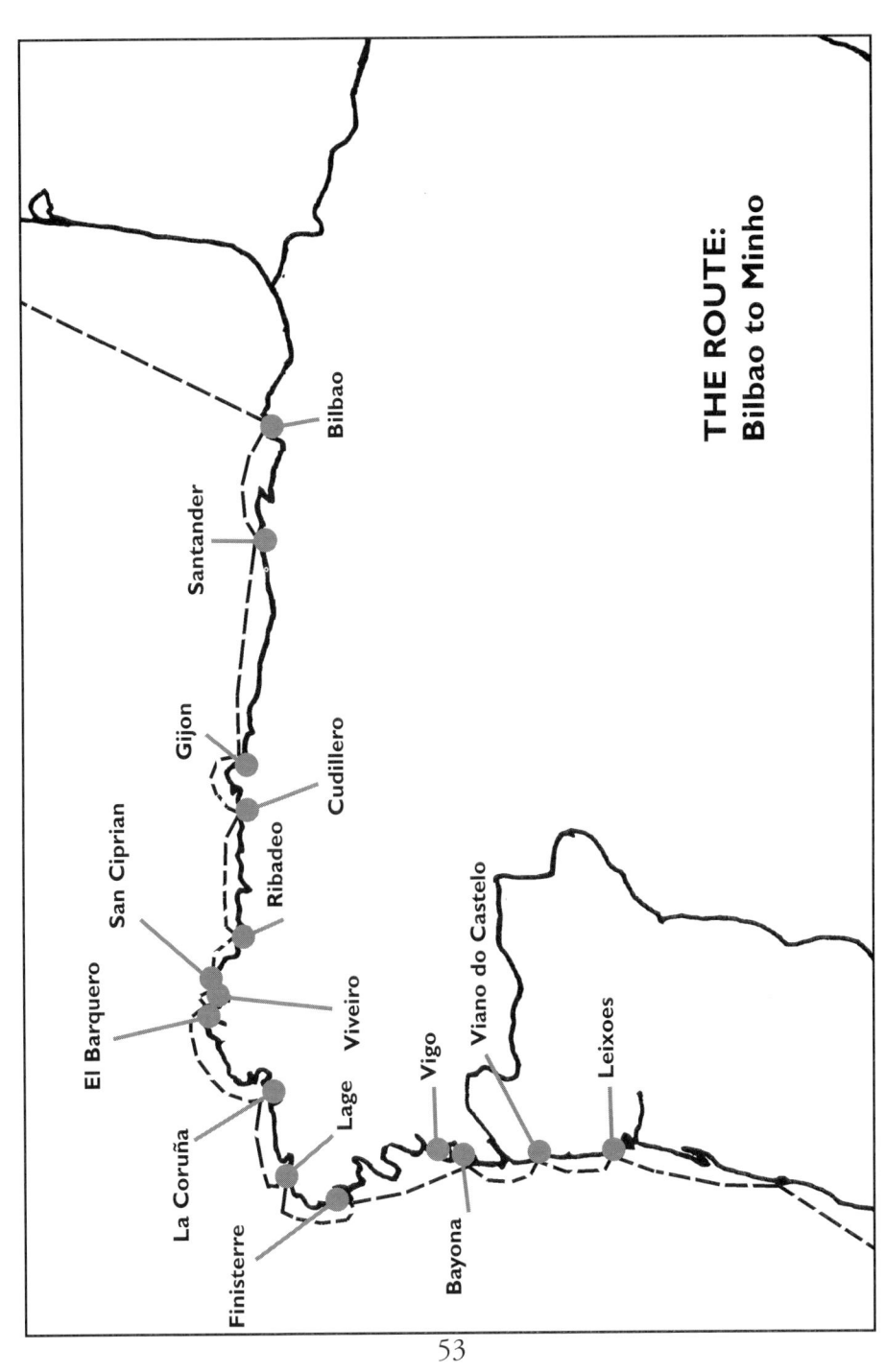

Chapter Six

Headwinds and grey days north of Spain

NOW JON had left, we needed to do some shopping and laundry, and one of the drawbacks of Getxo marina is that it takes 20 minutes to walk to the nearest small supermarket and you need a taxi to go to the large supermarket. We wanted some exercise and so chose to walk to the small supermarket which took us through a very pleasant and up-market residential area. The supermarket was actually quite good. Loaded down with bags we looked for some lunch and discovered what the locals in the area do on Saturdays. They just mob all the little bars that sell tapas, eat snacks, drink and chat. If there is not enough room inside, then they do it on the pavements, as noisily and happily as Spaniards know how.

The Leisurely Route to the Med

We found some nice baguettes in a restaurant called Krunk, and walked back to the marina. Now we were in Spain, there were more hours in the day. You can get up late, have a leisurely lunch at 2-4pm followed by a siesta, and still have plenty of time to take the Metro into Bilbao for dinner.

We wanted to move on the next day, so we did not spend much time in the city, which is now famous for the stunning Guggenheim museum. Bilbao also hits the headlines because it is the biggest city in the troubled Basque region.

The Metro was excellent; fully automated and very cheap. It took 20 minutes to the centre of the city. We had the address of a vegetarian restaurant and now saw much of the centre of Bilbao as we tried to track it down. There were wide streets lined with grand buildings and large traffic-filled plazas. Each time we asked for directions we got closer to our target until eventually, at nearly ten o' clock, there was the restaurant.

In the UK, of course, there could be a problem getting served at that time, but not in Spain. Unless the restaurant caters for foreign tourists don't bother to arrive before 9pm; it probably won't be open. Spaniards consider it normal to arrive for dinner at 10 or 11pm or even later.

We had a good dinner, and then headed back to the station, somewhat concerned that the timetable we had seen did not indicate the time of the last train on Friday and Saturday nights. Then it dawned on us: they run all through the night because people want to go home at any time! In fact, we did not get back to the marina until 1am where the bars were heaving with revellers, and they were still arriving in droves!

On Sunday it was sunny again for most of the time, with a temperature of about 25 deg C. We had a quiet day in and around the marina and walked along the beach—lots of people of all shapes and sizes were sunbathing topless—and up to an old fishing village which was delightful. From the top of the hill above the village we had a marvellous view of the bay and the harbour.

The port of Bilbao is really built in a natural harbour or ria, which is a wide but fairly short estuary like the Carrick Roads at Falmouth, or Plymouth Sound. This was the first of many we were to see along the Spanish coast, although most are on the coast of Galicia in the north-west corner. This one is like a bay that is longer than it is wide, enclosed by steep cliffs either side. There is a narrow river that runs inland to Bilbao, but the ria really ends in the curved seawall well before the city.

It is not an attractive ria, partly because of the docks and their cranes but also because there is a large industrial complex nearby. Getxo is clearly the best part of the area, and the little fishing village on the hill, which has its own little harbour is very attractive. It has a tiny square, shaded by trees, several small restaurants, including one serving Mexican food, and small houses separated by narrow alleys. None of the alleys are wide enough to be called streets. Above the village are blocks of flats, however.

Most of the bars around the marina or by the beach are expensive, as you might expect. During the day, we watched what was happening in the marina. For the most part, the Spaniards around Bilbao seem to go to their boats on Sundays—or they may have sailed over from the next port—and invite their friends to visit them which they do, dressed in their best clothes. Many of the women were wearing summer dresses and high heeled shoes, and it was clear that this was the way to spend Sunday afternoon. Those without boats promenade beside the water or sit at tables outside bars and cafés chatting enthusiastically—this is one of the major Spanish pastimes, which is such a delight to see because they are so obviously enjoying themselves.

21st June: Headwinds and swell for the short passage to Santander

We intended to move on the next morning, but when we poked our heads out of the main hatch we had a shock—it was raining and visibility was poor. We decided to wait and see if it would improve. We had enjoyed two weeks of sunny weather and felt that we were far enough south to expect sunshine for the rest of the voyage; it was late June, after all. We knew that they had quite a lot of rain in the north of Spain, but thought it fell mainly in the winter. Maybe we were wrong and those lovely mountains attract the rain at any time. We went up to the office and asked about the weather.

'I have a problem with the weather forecast,' the manager told us with a frown, as he stared at the screen of his computer. 'It comes on the Internet. Today, I am looking at the screen a long time, but nothing comes.'

Definitely good value, that man. Anyway the forecast did come a bit later, and they were expecting a north or north-easterly wind of force two to four, which would do very nicely thank you. As we waited for the weather to clear, Pauline baked a loaf of bread using one of those packs which contains all the ingredients.

By noon, the weather was clearing up, so we set off—there was still time to reach Santander. As we headed out to sea we met a steep swell but instead of helping us, as it had to date, it was right on the nose! Despite the forecast, so was the wind—a less friendly north-westerly instead of the north-easterly we had been promised.

As the wind was stronger than we had expected we reefed two panels. We had just done so, when there was a big blast on a horn, and still quite some distance away was the P&O ferry heading out for Portsmouth. We turned off to port a little and then continued on our way. Once we had passed the last breakwater, the swell was not quite so bad, but was ever present. As we were heading into the wind, we motor-sailed. It remained cloudy for most of the day, but we nevertheless were able to enjoy the beautiful coastline of golden yellow beaches between high cliffs and mountains that roll down to the sea.

Pauline had been busy with the camcorder, first filming the P&O ferry and then the mountains, which she knew her parents would enjoy. Then as we approached Lareda, a fishing port where there is also a marina, there was more of interest. First, a yacht came out, and made its way along the coast, whereas we were three or four miles out to sea so that we would clear the headland just past Lareda. Then, a couple of large fishing boats appeared out of the entrance, followed by a few more, and a few more. Altogether about ten large fishing boats came out and headed off north-east. It was about four o'clock so we presumed that they needed to get to a distant fishing ground by dark. As they passed us they pitched and wallowed, rising up on the waves then half disappearing in the troughs, showing just how big the waves were. Pauline captured this on video for her parents:

'These waves will impress them,' she said.

Later on we were sailing in a westerly direction, and as the wind had dropped a little we shook out the reefs, but spent most of the day motor-sailing, which was a real change from when we had been sailing down the

Headwinds and grey days north of Spain

French coast. Near Santander, the hills are lower than around Bilbao, and the entrance is quite unusual, without any landmarks to the east. Near the west side of the river mouth is a tall rocky island, with an isolated rock to the north. Further to the west, there are some cliffs and hills, but to the east there are beaches and sand dunes which come close to the channel.

Once in the river, we soon passed a sheltered bay in which you can anchor but decided to go to the yacht club, because both this bay and the marina are quite a long way from the town, the marina being well down the river. According to the pilot books, you can go into the harbour of the yacht club if there is room. When we went in, we could see some spaces but decided to raft up against a large fishing boat and then ask in the club. However, no sooner had we done so when one of those security guards that are employed widely in Spain came along and told us to get out and go on a buoy.

We shrugged our shoulders and went. As we looked for a suitable buoy, we passed a small yacht on one of the buoys and, not only did it fly the red ensign, but it had a junk rig! No one was aboard. We found a suitable buoy just opposite the club, which is a plain rectangular white building on stilts, actually in the river, joined to the bank by a concrete bridge.

A little later a small inflatable came out from the club to Zefka. On board were the crew from the junk-rig yacht, *Corida*. Pete, the owner, was on his way to Cyprus with a friend who was crewing on his first voyage. Their boat was a Virgo Voyager, a 23-footer, which was by far the smallest boat we met undertaking such a voyage. *Corida* has an enormous sail; the size you would expect on a 28-footer.

They had come directly from Audierne in three days, and at times had been surfing down the waves at eight knots, covering over 100 miles each day which is very good going for such a small boat. Pete did admit that the sail was so large that he had to reef very early indeed or the boat got out of control.

The same Frenchman who had visited us in Audierne to enquire about our rig visited them too. They were also paid a visit by the customs who warned them against sailing down the coast owing to all the firing. They were planning to go on to Gijon the next day after lunch, and sail overnight. We had an interesting discussion about rigs.

The Leisurely Route to the Med

A little later a large black inflatable came alongside to collect our fee, and confirmed that he could take us ashore. So we asked him to come at nine the following morning so that we could use the clubhouse showers and go into the town. We planned to spend the day there, and leave during the following night, since there was really nowhere we could stop before Gijon, about 80 miles further on. There are two ports on the way, Ribadasella and Llanes, but you need to enter near high water, and that was not practical the day that we would be passing them. However, if we left really early, we would be off these ports at around high water should some bad weather blow in. Another possibility is Suances, actually a private port partway up a river serving a factory, and it has the same limitations as the others.

Incidentally, when making any coastal passage it is a good idea to decide not only where you are heading, but where you can go if the weather turns nasty en route. I made a routine of checking possible ports of refuge, and it paid dividends later on.

The clubhouse of the Santander yacht club, probably built in the 1950s, is quite grand, with lots of dark wood panelling. It has a large hall and a wide staircase with polished wood banisters leading up to an impressive restaurant and a balcony where you can sit, with a drink, overlooking the river. There is also a snooker room. All the facilities at the club are good. The showers are down below where the arrangement for disposing of their waste was rather novel; just holes in the floor, for the water to pour through into the river below.

We enjoyed the part of Santander we saw—the area near the clubhouse and ferry terminal. First we found a very busy bar for breakfast—it always pays to go to busy bars. This one was not only popular, but was unusual in that the customers included a large number of women, some with young children. In most towns in Spain you see very few women in the bars. One man came in, downed a large brandy and disappeared, and this at 10am. That is quite common in Spain, but as Pauline remarked, not a welcome sight when you are eating your breakfast.

We posted the second video cassette home, then bought cherries, apricots, carrots and some of those long, thin green peppers which are so much nicer than the thick, hard ones sold in the UK at an outside market.

Beside the stalls for fruit and vegetables, some second-hand goods were spread out on the ground. The vendors' children, very poorly dressed, sat among the bric-a-brac.

Just around the corner was a little stall selling olives. We bought some of the large, delicious *Gordal* olives which we found first in Seville, and later bought some long sticks of wholemeal bread in a little baker's shop nearby. Much more fun than tackling Tesco.

Later we wandered around the streets and found several large squares, some wide streets and further away from the port, many narrow ones. Some parts of the town are quite hilly, and most of the shops are small; some very basic, and others very stylish and up-market, but with a wide range of merchandise.

One of the best investments we made was in a couple of bowls, which are large enough to contain a salad, pâté or whatever and chunks of bread—in other words lunch. I had got fed up with retrieving bits of salad or bread from the cockpit sole as the boat rolled when we were having lunch on the move. We found that these were just ideal, and used them for lunches and some other meals as well after that.

One of the highlights of the morning was our visit to a large *ferreteria* or ironmonger, whose shop extended over three floors. We were still searching for a 12mm drill with a 10mm shank. It appeared that tools were sold on the second floor, so we climbed the rickety stairs which led to the first floor, just a gallery around the four walls packed with saucepans, coffeemakers and every conceivable domestic utensil. From there you could look down to the floor below. We persevered, going up another flight of old wooden stairs to where it looked as if tools were sold. I joined the queue, only to be sent down to the ground floor when I explained what I wanted.

Downstairs, all sorts of people from tradesmen to old ladies, wanting everything from specially shaped hammers and other tools to saucepans, were being served or waiting. We settled down for a long wait, when the man from the second floor came down and muttered something into the ear of the manager, and suddenly we were being served—getting priority because we had already done our fair share of queuing, we supposed.

The Leisurely Route to the Med

I explained what I wanted, and the assistant went off to one of the many little drawers and produced a drill with a plain shank. I explained again, and eventually he returned with the very thing. And then, he told me the price in English! A fascinating place, with a fantastic stock including such items as milking machines and automatic drinking troughs for cattle all crammed into the small, square three-storey shop.

Not many restaurants in Santander cater for vegetarians—or in Spain as a whole for that matter—but there was supposed to be just one vegetarian restaurant in the town. We were given directions to it but, although several people we asked thought they knew where it was, we were unable to find it. Presumably it has closed or moved. Instead we found a really nice bar in one of the grand squares in the city where we could have a vegetable sandwich sitting outside just beneath the cloisters that provide shade, and make the buildings look much more interesting.

When we returned to the yacht club we asked at the reception desk for a weather forecast.

'Ah yes,' said the man on duty. He came out from behind the counter and pointed to a small notice board with the word Meteo printed on a piece of paper at the top. It was quite empty.

'This is where it is,' he said, pointing to the empty board. 'But we expect it in half an hour or so.'

At that a British man came up, also looking for a weather forecast. His boat was *Annabel*, a Southerly 115, which is about 38 feet long and is unusual in that it has a swing keel. He was due to leave quite soon with his hired crew, heading for Mallorca.

'I want to get there as soon as I can,' he said, 'and establish a base there.' He sounded just like a businessman about to set up a branch somewhere, and everything had to be done in a hurry. Still, he seemed a very pleasant man.

'Where is your boat moored?' he enquired.

'Out on a buoy in front of the club. We went into the marina, but were turned out by a security guard,' I replied.

'Well, we just went in, found a space and moored the boat. Then I came in here and told them, and they said it was OK.'

Headwinds and grey days north of Spain

Obviously, the answer is to arrive when the staff are on duty. Actually, it was not bad on the mooring, especially since they run a service to and from the boats there. However, the shape of the river is such that every so often some quite large waves come along.

We went upstairs and had a relaxing coffee on the verandah overlooking *Zefka*, the river and the hills beyond. By now it was very windy. The dinghies sailing in front of the clubhouse kept capsizing, and the crew of a small yacht were having fun as it heeled over at a tremendous angle—and it only had its mainsail up. There was no sign of *Corida*, the junk-rig Voyager, and we did not see her again. We learned later that *Corida* had gone into Suances—and received a great welcome—and later spent some time cruising around the rias. She had arrived at the border between Portugal and the south of Spain in August, where the owner had temporarily left her in the marina there.

The inflatable took us back to the boat where I worked out the passage plan to Gijon. So long as the weather was not too bad we decided to leave at about 2am, so that we would arrive at Gijon at around six in the evening. That meant it was definitely time for a siesta. That evening we were supposed to eat and get to bed early, but did not succeed, so we had had about three hours sleep at the most before waking to prepare to sail away.

23rd June: Buzzed by customs—twice—and then by a fishing boat. After that, plain sailing to Gijon

We were ready to leave at 2.15am and, since there was just a gentle easterly breeze, we raised the mainsail on the buoy before setting off. We could see the way to the main channel clearly, and thereafter we steered between the red and green lights until we were opposite the island near the river mouth. Just before reaching the island we saw a motor launch of some sort heading along the coast inside the island very fast. Now, suddenly we were floodlit; the launch was directing a pair of very strong lights straight at *Zefka*. Presumably it was a customs launch. Having ruined our night vision, it went off leaving us to concentrate on following the channel. It was then, just as our eyes were adjusting to the dark again, that we saw the small rock just to the north of the Isla de Torre—Island of the Tower—as they call the big island. The rock is quite unlit, and just where you might think of turning west.

The Leisurely Route to the Med

We continued to follow the course out to sea, and a little later another launch appeared. This one did not bother to approach us, but just shone his bright lights at us from a distance. We wondered whether the customs are always that vigilant, or whether they were looking for a particular vessel.

Soon afterwards we were cruising along the coast, four or five miles out, and could see that the lights of Santander actually extend a long way along the coast. After that we saw the lights of a few small villages as we passed and could just make out the entrance to Suances. By four o' clock it seemed very cold, and we put on some extra layers of clothing, despite the very light wind.

An hour or so later, a breeze sprung up from the south-west. This was unexpected since the forecast we had received over the Navtex indicated a north-easterly wind would be coming. Some mariners swear by the British forecasts, and others by the French; maybe Spaniards rely on Spanish forecasts. Nevertheless accurate weather forecasts do not seem easy to obtain on the north coast of Spain wherever they come from. We were relying on whatever we obtained on the Navtex, over the VHF radio, in marina offices or from other sailors. We received few forecasts over the VHF until we came into the range of Finisterre, so what information we had came mostly from the Navtex.

It was just beginning to get light when a really bizarre incident occurred; it still puzzles us to this day. We saw a fishing vessel about a quarter of a mile away which was heading almost parallel with us in the opposite direction. Suddenly, it turned toward us, and we could see both his red and green navigation lights and his white steaming light. We altered our course to starboard so that we would be out of his way, although we could see that the boat was travelling too fast to be trawling. After we had changed course, the vessel followed suit and continued to head straight for us in a menacing manner.

Next, he switched on an amber flashing light on the cabin roof of the vessel, and finally he turned his large searchlight full on us. We turned off course even further, somewhat mystified, and after a few minutes the vessel went away. What was all that about? Just plain cussedness or an anti-

Brit, or did he really think we might spoil his fishing? We have heard that Spanish fishing vessels threaten smaller foreign fishing vessels in this manner, but in no way did we resemble a fishing vessel of any type. A mystery.

It was not until after six that you could say the day had dawned, even though this was the shortest night of the year. We had both stayed on watch through the night, but now Pauline went down for a couple of hours' sleep. By 7.30am I was feeling really drowsy, but the presence of some fishermen's floats and a few fishing boats helped keep me alert. We had not seen many floats of fishermen's pots for some time, and had been sailing well off the coast during the night to ensure that we avoided them. However, we did see quite a number that day, and from then onwards. Some were in 150 metres of water, so it really was necessary to keep a good lookout.

As is not uncommon, by the time I went down for a nap, I felt wide awake but did manage to sleep for an hour or so, and came up much refreshed. That day the coastline continued to delight us. There were no more sandy beaches but cliffs and foothills with mountains behind. There were a few spectacular inlets into the cliffs, and one or two areas where big hills rose up from a narrow plain or low foothills. In such an area a little village would nestle below the foothills. Llanes is one village like that, and as we passed, about seven miles off, the wind increased a little, but it was still necessary to motor-sail.

So it was that in the early evening we were approaching Gijon when we saw what looked like a big rectangular block in the sea ahead. Even after she had studied it with the binoculars, Pauline was sure it was the end of the jetty. However, the 'jetty' was heading toward us at a good speed. When we altered course we could see that it was one of those modern container ships which are essentially a long, flat deck with a block of flats for the crew at the stern. Pauline filmed the huge vessel as it steamed past.

Gijon is a large commercial port with a wide entrance, in fact it is so wide that it is quite difficult to be sure you are in the right place! The commercial harbour is well over to the west of the city, whereas the marina is slightly to the east. The first time you approach from the east it is quite

The Leisurely Route to the Med

difficult to make out which bay you should enter, particularly if it is hazy as it was when we arrived. The first bay actually leads into a beach only, and you need to clear a headland in front of the town and head toward the commercial port before turning in to avoid some rocks which are shown by a green beacon. Once you have turned round the headland it is plain sailing.

The trickiest part of the day usually comes at the end of a long passage, when you are feeling tired, and tend to relax because you are approaching a harbour—it is then that you need to be extra alert. Of course, pilot books and charts are a tremendous help in approaching and entering strange ports, but the situation is rarely exactly as you expect it. There are usually some anxious moments before the way becomes clear. Then, when you enter the marina itself you wonder whether there will be a space, where you will need ropes and fenders and so on.

On this occasion the wind was the problem—we had visited the marina by car and so had a rough idea of the layout. The wind, after a day of promising much but achieving little, chose to blow strongly as we approached the reception pontoon and blew at right angles to the very short and wobbly finger pontoon making if difficult to moor.

After that little excitement, I went into the office and signed in quite quickly, but I was then told to visit customs. Yes, we all are supposed to be in the EU now, and in any case we had come from a Spanish port, but nevertheless at Gijon this is what you must do. I went next door into a characterless building with a high ceiling, and eventually they found the officer, who led me into a dreary little office where we sat down opposite sides of a desk. The officer produced a set of forms which were just the same as the ones I had filled in at Santander and left on the club reception desk. However, I was not to be allowed to fill them in myself and so save time. Instead, the officer had a master form with the relevant words in each box in English. He would ask me one word and I would tell him the answer, helping him in Spanish. We went through this procedure in a painfully slow manner until at last I was told I could go. We were to find a similar situation in Portugal, and I suppose that they have so many customs officers with nothing to do, now they are not required at borders and airports, that they have to employ them somewhere.

Headwinds and grey days north of Spain

I returned wearily to the boat, shaking my head at bureaucracy, and we went to find a berth; you have to do that for yourself at Gijon. The visitors' marina, which is quite separate from that for locals, had very few boats in it, so we decided to head for the side of the first pontoon where there was plenty of room behind. That would make it easy for *Zefka* to go out astern. But it wasn't going to be simple. Pauline continues:

'The strong wind was still having fun as I took my position on the starboard deck ready to make a quick jump for the pontoon to secure the warps. We passed behind a boat—which turned out to be *Annabel*, whose skipper we had met in Santander—and when *Zefka* turned in toward the pontoon she seemed to be moving a little faster than usual, as the wind was now right behind. There were two men standing on the pontoon and, anticipating our needs they were already on their way to take our ropes and hold the bow. Then, I realised that one of them was Ken!'

'Ken is the large, friendly, knowledgeable guy whose yacht was moored next to ours in Plymouth Yacht Haven! This was the second time that he had turned up unexpectedly. The first time was when, at the end of my VHF radio course, he turned out to be the examiner.'

On this occasion he seemed to materialise out of thin air. In fact, Ken had told us before we left that he was taking a boat down to the Med in the summer and we now knew that the boat was *Annabel*. He had joined her at Santander for the rest of the voyage—just the man to have in the crew, I imagine.

We had a chat with him and the skipper a little later. The skipper told us:

'They are talking about force seven winds in the west of Galicia and I want to head onto La Coruña early tomorrow, so I am not sure what we will do.'

They had gone by the time we got up the next day, and needless to say we did not see them afterwards. However, we did catch up with *Annabel*; the following February we found her out of the water at Almerimar, in the south of Spain.

There was a festive air in Gijon that evening as they prepared to celebrate the longest day in true Spanish style. The man in the marina office told us that the festivities would take place on the beach near the marina, but we were just too, too tired, after being up from 1.30am. We had something to eat and went to bed. Soon after midnight we were awakened by tremendously loud fireworks exploding one after another almost like machine gun fire from a beach near the marina. After a brief silence, we heard more distant fireworks coming from the beach on the other side of the town, as if in reply. This went on for some time and, just when we thought that fireworks don't come any louder, the noise built up to an even louder crescendo and it was over. The silence that followed was short-lived: Spanish music, piped all round the marina and sea front continued through the night but we were so tired we went back to sleep.

We spent a day in the town before moving on. It was a beautiful, hot and cloudless day as we set out for the town. In the nearby tourist office we learned that there was a vegetarian restaurant called Santo Remedio in the old town, and also a few health food shops, so we were able to buy some useful foodstuffs. Gijon was definitely worth tarrying in a little. It has some nice parks, a large beach, and the old town with attractive old buildings and narrow streets.

We found Santo Remedio in time for a light lunch, eaten outside, and returned there for dinner, which was served in a delightful blue-walled room on the second floor. In fact, the restaurant had been started only three weeks earlier by two women, one with a medical background, the other with a business background. The businesswoman was a real character. Buxom, well-groomed and about 40, she spent at least half an hour explaining to one group of people what had happened when they had the building revamped—so far as I could gather—and her words led to frequent outbursts of laughter. Eventually she took their order, and her description of the menu was very animated and obviously humorous. We enjoyed the scene, and our meal.

In preparation for sailing the next day, we refuelled for the first time since Les Sables d'Olonne. The combination of a large fuel tank and economical diesel engine were quite an advantage on this sort of voyage—fuel is not available in many of the smaller ports. In Spain you are not allowed to buy the pink fuel supplied for the fishing boats, but instead the diesel fuel sold for cars—Gasole A. The small fishing ports stock only Gasole B, and it is only in the larger marinas that you can buy Gasole A.

In Gijon we met some interesting folk, such as Bob, with his Proctor 33, and Nikki and Ron on *Avanti,* a Westerly 33. We did not see much of the owners of *Saxon Warrior,* who were headed in the opposite direction, but everyone else was talking of getting to La Coruña. When you are along this section of the coast this is the target that overrides all else. It is not just that La Coruña is a big port in a well-sheltered ria, but that the weather along the Galician coast can be wild, and once you are in La Coruña you are past the worst of it.

Bob had sailed from Audierne to Gijon single-handed. Various of his friends had volunteered to crew for him on other parts of the voyage, but none wanted to go across the Bay of Biscay! He had relied on the radar, set to 16 miles, to tell him whether there were any ships nearby, and checked it every 15 minutes. Needless to say, by the time he arrived in Gijon he was very exhausted, and not keen to see the Bay of Biscay again. A couple were to join him further on for the next leg.

25th June: Plans upset by heavy weather; we ended up in a good harbour where you're not really welcome—but it was free.

Bob said that he thought he would head off the same day as us, but *Avanti* was the first boat to leave at about half past seven in the morning with grey cloud overhead. After checking the weather forecast, we followed just after nine, and left Bob with his engine already running. Bob was hard on our heels and motor-sailing a little faster than us in a heavy swell. Once we reached the headland near Gijon—Cabo Penas—we were sailing against the current, against a westerly wind, and against the swell. Because the Bukh 24hp engine is a little small for *Zefka*, progress was slow, and at times the engine was only driving us forward at three knots. *Zefka* bucked and dived into the waves, with water streaming all along the decks, but we kept dry in the cockpit, and the motion was not too bad. Bob had nosed past us, using the full power of his much larger engine, and we remained in close company for some time.

It was clear that with the wind on the nose and the swell from the north-west, we were not making enough progress to reach Ribadeo in reasonable time that evening; we were averaging 3-4 knots. Bob's Proctor was bucking wildly, and hardly going any faster. We decided to head for Cudillero, a small fishing port where there are a few pontoons. There is a prominent lighthouse near the entrance, and the harbour wall is quite clear once you are within about half a mile. Although we had not discussed our plans with Bob, we saw him head in first, which made life easier for us. We watched him turning round the breakwater, which gave us a good idea of where the entrance was. The Seafile told us that once past the breakwater we would have to turn sharply to the right, and indicated that the entrance was very narrow indeed.

There was still a heavy swell running as we approached the harbour entrance, but subsided as we got close. Soon afterwards, we met an old man rowing a wooden dinghy straight out from the harbour. We waved as we went past, and he waved back enthusiastically, which was encouraging. We headed for the middle of the gap and turned round the breakwater, keeping well clear because we could see that the entrance was actually very wide. On the left hand side we could see the old harbour, now deserted, and the village up in the valley that runs down to the sea. It looked a charming little place.

We proceeded into the harbour along a fairly wide channel, keeping a watchful eye on a cluster of rocks on one side, and rejoiced in the calmness of the water. We could see the fishing boats and a shipyard ahead, all protected by this very high and long breakwater, and then some pleasure craft and pontoons came into view. There appeared to be a few empty spaces on one pontoon. We could see *Avanti* at one end of the pontoon, and the Proctor near the landward end. I turned in, and at first thought that the space next to *Avanti* might be the best, but as we approached we could see a rope across the pontoons to prevent anyone entering. In fact, most of the moorings had these dark ropes across just above the water level where they were difficult to see, so care is needed here—and entering in the dark is not recommended.

Then I realised that we had a reception committee. I could see Bob on the pontoon, and another man, who from the distance could easily have been the marina manager. So we headed toward them, and moored starboard onto the pontoon right next to the Proctor. It turned out that the other man was Ron, the skipper of *Avanti*. After we had moored, he told me that he and his wife had sailed out of Plymouth for several years,

Headwinds and grey days north of Spain

but they had bought the Westerly because his wife wanted a boat with a more traditional interior than the Freedom he had had previously. They were on their way south, but they had tried to do so the previous year.

'The weather was so bad that we just got fed up with waiting for a suitable day to come south,' he said. 'In the end, we decided to cruise round Brittany and then headed back home.' They live in south Wales, and now they were making their second attempt.

'When we were out there we realised that we would not get to Ribadeo until after 1am, and I didn't want to go in there in the dark. So we came here,' Ron explained. He pointed to a yacht rafted up to another boat on a permanent mooring nearby.

'They came from Gijon and arrived before us,' he said.

I looked across and saw a white boat with a green stripe along the hull that I remembered seeing in Gijon. It was called *L'Albatros*, and it had a long low hull.

Cudillero is only about 30 miles from Gijon, so when we arrived there was plenty of time to go ashore, even though it would be a long walk to the village. We walked up the gangplank only to find that there were two gates and each was locked and surrounded by a large wire frame making it impossible to get past. We were too lazy to get the dinghy out and blow it up, so we stayed on board and had an early night. At any rate, no one came and asked us to pay for being imprisoned on the pontoon.

We were unable to get any sort of weather forecast, but Bob had a Roberts multi-band radio on which he could receive Radio 4 from the UK. We tried to get Radio 4 on our car radio/cassette player in the boat, but we got two or three stations speaking at the same time. He said that he would listen to the weather forecast at 5.50am, and so long as the forecast was reasonable would set off immediately.

'I found when I came down as a crew in another boat last year that if you start early, you usually get four or five hours before the wind and swell get up, so you can cover quite a lot of ground that way,' he told us.

We found that Bob was worth listening to as he has plenty of sailing experience and has done a lot of skippered chartering. We later found that he had sailed over 25,000 miles.

'As you pushed us off this morning, we'll help you off the pontoon tomorrow morning,' Pauline said.

Bob seemed quite cheered.

'Thanks,' he said. 'When I bought this boat—and after I'd handed over the cheque—they told me that when manoeuvring the only thing to do was to see where she was going and help her go there. They were right. She doesn't go where I want her to astern at all,' he said.

26th June: Less wind than forecast—and less swell as we made our way to the charming ria and town of Ribadeo

We did manage to hear the weather forecast from the BBC, and Bob confirmed it was for a force four to five from the south-west. A few minutes later we helped him manoeuvre off the pontoon, and we could see that his boat was a bit of a handful, but that he was in control. We took his advice about the weather, and left about an hour later, just before eight. As we passed *Avanti*, Nikki and Ron looked up in surprise and asked what weather forecast we had heard.

'The BBC is forecasting four to five from the south-west,' we said.

'Oh,' said Nikki. '*L'Albatros* heard the French forecast and it is five to six from the north-west with thundery showers. They told us that the village is very nice, so we are staying.'

'I think we'll go on. We'll have to see whether the British or French are right,' I said. 'It isn't too far. Less than 50 miles, I think.'

We bade them farewell, and even though we stopped for several days at various ports, we did not see them again until the winter. This was not surprising because they spent quite a bit of time cruising around the rias before going south, and did not arrive in the Med until the autumn.

We had a lovely view of the pretty village bathed in the early morning sun as we passed. Bob's forecast of flat seas in the morning proved correct. There was neither wind nor swell as we motored at our usual five knots. For two or three hours there was very little wind, and the sky remained overcast. We passed dozens of small fishing boats in the still sea in one of the bays, and went on our way passing low cliffs and mountains. Unfortunately it was cloudy and the summits of many of the mountains were in haze. Visibility was not good until we were close to Ribadeo.

Headwinds and grey days north of Spain

By 11am the south-westerly wind was strong enough for us to switch the engine off, but then dropped to almost nothing at lunchtime. Then guess what? It went around to the north-west, and remained there for a couple of hours before dropping, and it finished the day blowing from the west. So, neither weather forecast was correct—or both were correct—and we ended up motor-sailing.

Ribadeo is about a mile inside a long and interesting ria, but there is quite a large town with a lighthouse about five miles to the east and this can easily be mistaken for Ribadeo. After that, a little care is needed to go far enough past the mouth of the ria before turning almost south, and then lining up a couple of markers on the hills on the east bank. When you can see a pair of markers near the marina, which is just past the road bridge, you turn through almost 90 degrees. These proved difficult to see. We could see a short white tower at the end of the marina which could have been one of them, and it is only when I was thinking 'We really must turn now' that I saw a couple of red diamonds lining up—rather faintly on small white boards.

With a couple of hours till high water, I knew there should be plenty of water as far as the marina, and there was. Later, as we motored down parallel with the high breakwater we saw a number of masts the other side, so it looked as if that was where visitors moored. When we turned into the marina, we could see the visiting yachts there against the wall but no spaces – we would have to raft up. The biggest boat was a pale blue yacht of about 40 feet, and we chose her. When we pulled alongside, there was just one person on board. Helpful and welcoming, she took the bow line while we sorted out the rest.

By the time we had moored, the skipper of our next door neighbour, which was called *Calico of Martlet*, had come back and suggested we take the lines back to *Zefka*. His wife had tied them off on her cleats. We readily agreed, and then had a chat about our experiences. They had been to Bayona and were now heading back, but were in no hurry to reach England. They had evidently done a lot of sailing, because he had visited Ribadeo first about 30 years previously on his way to the West Indies.

The Leisurely Route to the Med

'Earlier this month we were holed up around Cape Finisterre and La Coruña for about a week,' he told us. 'The wind just howled and howled, force seven or eight for days. I have never seen a boat heel over so much on the anchor before; it must have been heeling at 20 degrees and held like that for a lot of the time,' he said.

That was not much encouragement. For several days the weather forecast had been telling us of force seven around the westerly coast of Galicia, which we had just entered.

When we asked about the supermarket, Mr Calico drew a plan of how to get to Claudio, the nearest and largest. There was just time to rush up there for some much-needed provisions before they closed—it was a Saturday again, and virtually all shops in Spain are closed on Sundays. It was a long climb from the marina up to the town but then only a few minutes to the large supermarket. With bulging rucksacks, we walked into town for some dinner.

When we had been there previously, we had stayed at the Ros Mary Hostal, and had concluded that we would get as good a meal at the hostal as anywhere else. Ribadeo is a nice little town, with a park and some attractive buildings, but restaurants are pretty thin on the ground and, not surprisingly, none caters for vegetarians. We had been there on the evening of 5th January, which is the festival of three kings in Spain. It is the evening children receive their Christmas presents, and in each town there is a procession led by three men dressed as the three kings seated on a lorry. As the lorry chugs its way through the town the kings throw sweets to the children, and they end up at the town hall. There they ascend to the balcony and throw more presents out.

Reminding ourselves of that pleasant evening, we enjoyed our simple meal and an excellent bottle of Ribera del Duero red wine and were feeling fairly mellow as we walked down the hill to the marina. Back on the jetty we met Bob who had also enjoyed a good and cheap dinner with a bottle of wine in a little bar near the marina.

27th June: Pleasant harbour manoeuvres delayed us, and later we hit really bad weather.

The following morning, Mr *Calico* knocked us up at nine o' clock to ask if we would like to pirouette our boat around and put it against the wall now that there was an empty space.

'I'll help you do it,' he said. 'Then, we will be able to leave if we want to.'

We agreed, so I took a long line from the stern, past the bow and tied it on to the jetty. Then, we let all the other lines go and gave Mr *Calico* the bow line. We pushed the stern off, and watched as *Zefka* just drifted around helped with a push here or there. When she was almost at right angles to *Calico*, I went ashore and pulled on the long stern line, and the boat went right around. Much simpler than trying to manoeuvre on the engine. *Calico of Martlet* was turned around in the same way.

A little later, I was standing on the jetty looking down on *Zefka* wondering how to secure her mooring lines. This was not simple because sufficient slack is needed in the ropes to allow for the tide but the boat needs to be restrained fore and aft. Because the jetty was so high the normal methods wouldn't work. At this point, I did not know how long we would be staying—it would depend on the weather forecast. Mr *Calico*, who was standing beside me, was clearly reading my mind because he said:

'At the risk of telling Grandma how to suck eggs, would you mind if I told you a good way of tying the boat up in this situation?'

'Not at all,' I replied.

'Well, what you want is two ropes that are fairly tight to stop it moving out from the quay,' he said, and I nodded in agreement, 'and two very long ropes, one going forward and one aft. The three metres or so change in height with the tide will not have much effect on the long ropes because they are so long and because the movement is at right angles to them.'

I agreed. If the ropes were long enough, the fall in the tide would only tighten them up a few inches. The short ropes would not be affected because they would be more or less at right angles to the boat.

'I don't know if you have any better ideas, Bob?' he asked Bob who had just come along the jetty.

'No. That will work fine,' Bob agreed.

So I tied *Zefka* up in that way, and had a chat with Bob. He had decided to stay at Ribadeo. He liked the town and the marina and had found that his friends, who were flying into Santiago de Compostelo, could get a bus directly to the town. Also, I think that he was a little tired of sailing single-handed; not so much the sailing as the getting off and onto moorings. He told us that he was heading for Lagos, and would leave the boat there. He did not want to arrive there until around the third week in August, and in any case would have to wait another three days in Galicia for his friends to arrive.

We had a bit of a shock when we were making our toast for breakfast; the gas bottle ran out although we had only changed to a new one just before leaving Gijon a few days earlier. The previous bottle had lasted three weeks. Either we had been given a duff bottle or we had a leak somewhere. Now we had two empty bottles. We would not be able to get any gas at Ribadeo on Sunday so we thought we might as well move on and get some elsewhere if the weather forecast was not too bad.

When we were ready to leave, I went over to see Bob to give him my address. We had heard that the wind would be a force three to four from the south-west, which would suit us well, as we would be going north-west. Bob had heard of the possibility of a force seven in Finisterre on the BBC weather forecast, but was not sure whether that would affect the area where we were heading. Our planned destination was Viveiro, about 40 miles away.

Chapter Seven

Excitement off the north coast

THERE WAS hardly any wind when we left the marina, and we were very relaxed as we followed the markers out of the ria. Little did we realise that this would be one of the most exciting days of the voyage. We knew we were starting much later than we would have liked—about 11.30am, but were not concerned because the weather forecast seemed favourable. As soon as we turned past the headland into the open sea we found a slight wind. The bad news was that instead of the south-westerly that had been forecast, it was from the north-west; we would be heading north-west all the way. I cursed that we had not got away a couple of hours earlier, but was thinking only that it would be rather hard work. We were heading for Viveiro, a ria some 40 miles along the coast.

Quite often, we had spent the morning with very little wind, and then seen it increase between two and three o'clock. Today was different; the wind strengthened gradually from about noon. We were motoring but making only about four knots as we fought our way through the swell, which was not too bad at first, but soon increased, and then continued to increase all the time. As the wind strengthened, we put two reefs in each sail, and set about motor-sailing at 20 to 30 degrees off the wind. It might seem strange to motor-sail with reefs in the sails, but we had found that by motor-sailing this close to the wind, the sails did quite a lot of work, and that with the reefs in, the boat sailed more upright. With that extra drive, the speed increased and the boat's motion improved. And so it was that day.

By the early afternoon, both the wind and swell had increased appreciably, but we were motor-sailing along comfortably at about five and a half knots. A couple of hours later, the angle of heel was increasing, we were down to just three panels, and were moving ahead at six knots. With the increased swell, spray was repeatedly thrown back over the deck and was beginning to be whipped up on the crests of the waves. Dark clouds were coming in from the west hinting that the weather was likely to deteriorate rather than improve. By this time, Archie, as we call the autopilot, could not cope with the force on the tiller so I took the helm. We carried on like this for a while.

As Pauline says, she began to squeak:

'It's getting worse and worse. Look how the battens are bending.'

I looked up. She was right. The bendy battens, which are designed to bend to improve the airflow over the sails, were bending much further than usual.

'Let's take more sail down now! The waves are getting bigger and bigger, etc. etc.' Some people go quiet when they are scared, Pauline gets noisy!

Because there were some rocky islands off the coast, we were a few miles out. We did not have a long way to go, but the sea was getting steeper and the wind was whistling—perhaps this was the force seven that Bob had mentioned. It was obvious that we should seek an alternative haven to Viveiro—like now. The only alternative was San Ciprian which I had seen from the chart belonged to Alumina Espanola, and which looked a very secure haven. We had already seen the smelter belching forth fumes and smoke, and were only a few miles away. Pauline took the helm while I studied the chart.

THE ROUTE:
Viveiro & El Barquero

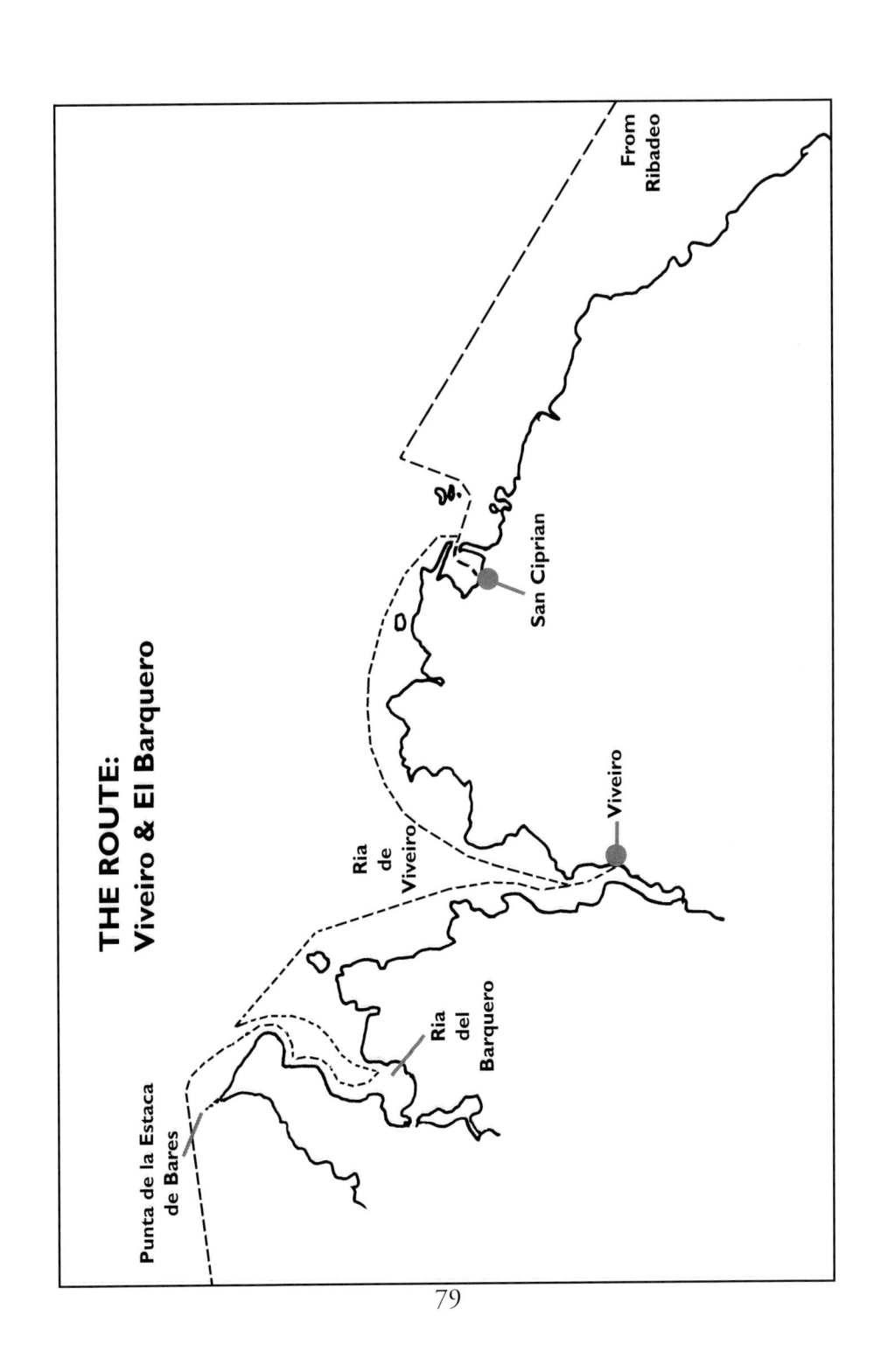

From Ribadeo

San Ciprian

Ria de Viveiro

Viveiro

Ria del Barquero

Punta de la Estaca de Bares

'We'll go into San Ciprian,' I said. 'It is a large harbour and it'll be sheltered by the headland. There must be plenty of room. We'll have to go round the rocks to get in.'

'OK', she said with a sigh of relief. I took the helm to turn *Zefka* around, tacking through the wind; we had actually passed the port, and now headed back and in towards the coast. As soon as *Zefka* was off the wind she started to fly off at great speed, surfing across the waves. So high was the swell breaking over the rocks in the middle of the bay, we could hardly see them. At this point Pauline suggested that she should take the helm so that I could study the chart, and as she did so I told her to aim just to the port of the rocks. Pauline was not very happy.

'We are heading straight for the rocks,' she shouted. 'Can't we go further away?'

'Don't worry,' I said. 'The wind is pushing us away from the rocks, and off to port there is deep water.'

She held the course, and *Zefka* raced on. Initially, the waves were making the boat corkscrew and every so often there was a large wave that threw the boat off course, putting an extra strain on the helmsman. Pauline worried that she would not be able to get back on course, especially since each time a big gust came, more effort than ever was needed to pull the tiller over to hold the boat on course; quite disconcerting when heading towards some extremely fierce looking rocks. When this happened I would push on the tiller to give some assistance.

After about 20 minutes of this buffeting, we could see rather more clearly, although the wind was howling as strongly as ever. Eventually, I could make out the yellow buoy, leaning over, and riding up and down on the waves.

'There's the buoy,' I shouted through the wind. 'You can now head away a little more from the rocks, and you will see it.'

By the time we passed the rocks they were giving us some shelter so both the swell and wind diminished. At last we could see the long, south breakwater protected by interlocking crosses of concrete, and the superstructure of a large cargo ship behind the breakwater.

Excitement off the north coast

Once we were in calm water, I thought that as a matter of courtesy I should call up the harbourmaster. I explained that we were seeking refuge, and he replied:

'Of course, you can stay here. Go anywhere you like. You will stay on the anchor?'

'Yes,' I replied. 'Thank you.'

We lowered the sails, and motored in between the breakwaters. Once inside, the sea was flat calm, and the wind was no longer a problem. We were in a large semicircular bay, with the jetty for cargo vessels on the left, and the smelter a little way further south from the jetty. There was a long sandy beach along half of the bay and then some rocks which separate the beach from a small cove with a few buildings. A few fishing boats and some dinghies were moored in the cove, which is called Puertino, and further around was the concrete breakwater. At the landward end of the breakwater was a tiny harbour where a French yacht was moored.

We decided to go over toward the beach and anchor there. Not having anchored previously on this voyage we took a little time finding a suitable spot in about six metres of water. It was then about seven o'clock, a couple of hours after high water. Once we had anchored, the relief was enormous. The sea was as calm as in a marina and, although we could hear the wind whistling, it seemed to be well over our heads. We had covered 33 miles in over seven hours but it seemed a good deal longer!

So far as we could see there was no town or village for several miles—people would not want to live right on top of the smelter—so we would have to eat on the boat. Without any gas it had to be a cold meal. We opened a tin of mixed pulses and made a bean salad which we ate with bread, fortunately still crisp. The meal proved to be surprisingly enjoyable.

Pauline takes up the tale:

'After dinner I went up on deck to video the scene. When we arrived there had been people on the beach enjoying the sunny day but now all was quiet and deserted. A gentle hum came from the aluminium works but was distant enough not to spoil the peace. There were hundreds of strange concrete shapes bolstering the sea wall, and many more were strewn casually about the hillside as if some giant had playfully thrown them there.'

The Leisurely Route to the Med

'The hillside in front of the boat was covered with pine trees, the moon just rising in the sky. All around us the water was still, but looking out through the harbour entrance I could see waves breaking on the rocky islands beyond, the only reminder of the day's rough sea. How good to be able to shelter when you need to. At that moment there was at least one yacht struggling across the Bay of Biscay trying to reach land and shelter. But we did not know about it then.'

'I went below and phoned my bank to enquire about the balance in my account. The woman on the other end could tell I was phoning from abroad and asked:

'Are you somewhere nice?'

'Oh yes,' I replied. 'We're anchored in a beautiful bay in the north-west of Spain.'

'How wonderful!' was her response.

Not fair of me really, but I didn't want to spoil it by telling her about the scary bit.'

28th July: The peaceful day after as we searched for gas in Viveiro—and heard of others' troubles.

The priority for the next day had to be to buy some gas, and since Viveiro was the biggest town in the area, that would be our destination, even though it was only about 12 miles distant. We started fairly early on a cold but clear morning—not unlike Cornwall at the same time of year—and had an easy passage to the entrance of the ria de Viveiro. Passing up this deep and fairly narrow inlet we enjoyed the rugged beauty all around as we headed for the town far inland. We had been told by one of the yachties we had met that 'if you go past the commercial port you have gone too far' at Viveiro, and that there was no room for visitors in the marina itself. We had also been told that there was one British boat that was resident in the marina, and to look out for large red mooring buoys.

Soon after passing the large breakwater which runs about half way across the ria, we saw an entrance to the fishing harbour and a commercial wharf on the south side. Therefore we turned into a large basin with fishing boats on the main breakwater, and a few on the opposite side—without looking at the Seafile. Further in we could see a number of small

Excitement off the north coast

boats moored near the beach, and a short pontoon where about 20 small boats were moored—with a light-blue British registered yacht on the end. This must be the place, we thought.

We circled around and could see one vacant buoy in a corner, and thought perhaps we should go there, out of everyone's way. But as we approached, a man working on a dinghy on the bank nearby signalled to us not to do so because there would not be enough water; according to the depth sounder there would be. Well, I think it always pays to listen to locals, so I went back to the main part of the harbour.

There was just one red buoy vacant there, right in the middle of the harbour, so we picked that up. A little later we were called up on the VHF radio by the British registered boat on the pontoon. It was called *Wild Goose*, and they wanted a weather forecast. We told them what we knew, which was not much; weather forecasts were few and far between on the Galician coast.

We went ashore in search of gas, and after pulling the dinghy up to the top of the beach, we met two of the three crew of *Wild Goose*. They had sailed across from Ireland in *Wild Goose*, which is one of those very pretty Nantucket Schooners, about 29 feet in length apart from the bowsprit, and very little freeboard. That was the first surprise: their boat was not the British resident we had expected to find.

The skipper, a young man, told us:

'We hit really bad weather in the Bay of Biscay and ended up going nowhere, and shipping water. We were in the shipping lanes as well. So we just had to heave-to for about two hours'.

They had been aiming for La Coruña but after two days of storms were blown so far off course that they had ended up here in the middle of the night, completely exhausted.

'It took us five days to get here. When we came in, we asked where we could moor, and the police said we could use their berth. That's how we came to be on the pontoon,' he explained. 'But we don't have a key, so we have to climb around the gate to get in and out.' They were three fit, young men, so that was not too much of a problem.

The Leisurely Route to the Med

Meanwhile, one of them was trying to get a weather forecast with his mobile from the British meteorological office at Bracknell. They had a forecast for today, but nothing for the next day. We left them to it, walked across the main road and into the nearest shop to ask where we could get gas.

'Not here,' the assistant replied. 'In Viveiro.'

That was the second surprise! It just shows that whatever people tell you, you should look in the pilot book.

'But where is this?' I enquired, somewhat mystified.

'Celeiro. Viveiro is down the road,' she said, pointing.

Now we knew why it didn't look like the Viveiro we had visited the previous winter! We thought that if we walked we might just get there before they closed for lunch, as it was not far. On the way we passed the new buildings erected for the fishing port at Celeiro and then we came to the real marina. It is true that there were no visitors on the pontoons, but in the basin were four red buoys, and a visiting yacht on each. So that is where we should have gone! But why we were told that we must not pass the commercial port, I don't know, because there is no port of any sort beyond the marina. Obviously there had been a misunderstanding.

We then passed a supermarket, and asked in the nearest bar where we could buy Camping Gaz. We were told it was just a few doors up. The barman came out, walked with us to the shop and pushed on the door. It was locked.

He looked at his watch, and saw that it was just after 1.30.

'They have gone to lunch,' he said. 'Back at 4.30.'

So we had three hours for lunch and to do some shopping in the supermarket. Viveiro is an interesting little town, with pleasant little squares and shopping alleys, so we spent a couple of hours easily enough. Some of the old buildings are very pretty, with rows of small windows in front of the balconies, but a few were decaying and derelict. We found a nice bar for lunch, but otherwise there was not much life in the town so, to kill time, we ended up eating doughnuts with coffee in the bar at the supermarket. The doughnuts were labelled 'sin colesterol' (without cholesterol). That made them almost healthy, didn't it? Eventually, we bought the Camping Gaz and took a taxi back to the boat.

Excitement off the north coast

It was a lovely hot day. From our buoy in the middle of the harbour we watched local children jumping into the water and swimming from steps near the pontoon. Several boys were using a rowing boat as a diving platform, ceaselessly diving off, then clambering back into the boat, never moving far from the shore.

We wondered whether someone might tell us to move off the buoy or at least ask for a mooring fee, but the only contacts we had with the locals were smiles and waves. There was a shipyard not far away from which the inevitable noises of hammering and machinery carried across the water. On the jetties the fishermen were busy preparing their boats for their night's work. Despite all this activity, it felt amazingly peaceful on our mooring.

That evening we managed to get the BBC weather forecast which we relayed to *Wild Goose*. They had moved off the pontoon and picked up a buoy nearby. They told us they planned to leave very early, and we planned to follow a little later. We were both heading toward La Coruña, about 60 miles away, although we were thinking we might stop in one of the rias on the way.

29th June: Ran into a near gale with helicopters, lifeboats—fortunately not for us—and sought shelter again

The alarm went off at 6.30am. As I opened the hatch to look at the weather, I caught sight of *Wild Goose* as she motored out of the harbour. It was a clear morning, but the sky was a pale pinkish yellow and there was some wind blowing already. We left just before 7am, and put the sails up almost as soon as we were past the breakwater. In the ria the wind seemed to be coming from the south-west, but it was hard to see how strong or whether it really would be a south-westerly because it was tumbling over the hills that enclosed the ria.

Neither of us is very good before breakfast, but we had left without any to save a bit of time. Pauline had hers when we were still in the ria, and the idea was that I should follow. When she came up we were approaching the small island of Coelleira, which separates Ria de Viveiro from Ria El Barquero. The sea was still fairly flat, but we could feel that the wind was strengthening, now coming more from the west, and we were in the lee of the island. At the moment I disappeared below decks,

The Leisurely Route to the Med

Pauline started calling for me to come up. Often it seems that, when Pauline is left in charge, the wind strengthens. So it was then, as she recounts:

'As we emerged from the lee of the island we were suddenly blasted by the wind howling in from the west and whipping up the sea as it went. Very soon we were doing over seven knots just off the wind across the entrance to El Barquero and with all our sail set it was very difficult to hold the tiller on course. I shouted to John. I think at first he thought I was overreacting, but as things started to fly about down below, he realised it was for real and came up into the cockpit.'

We immediately reefed one panel but, when we came out from the shelter of the hills to the west of the ria, the full force of the wind hit us and we had to reef again to just four panels. The wind was westerly so we were beating north-west toward the headland, but were not very close to the wind. *Zefka* was moving on well, despite the size of the swell.

As we looked ahead to the rocky peninsular we needed to pass, we were surprised to see a helicopter hovering above the rocks that stretch from the point into the sea. Many fishing boats were gathered near the rocks, and another one must have been stranded on them. Nearby was a bright orange lifeboat. Peering through the waves we were relieved to see that there was no light blue boat there, so it wasn't *Wild Goose* in trouble. Nevertheless, we hoped the people on board had been rescued safely, and we presumed this was the case because soon afterwards the helicopter left and the boats dispersed.

The waves were now at least two metres high, and although we were not heading directly into the wind, I realised that we would be doing so as soon as we turned around the headland, where the boat was in difficulties. It has a very long name—Punta de la Estaca de Bares. We had just decided to reduce sail again when we saw the lifeboat heading toward us, almost completely disappearing between each wave as it did so. It circled around us, but did not call us on the VHF radio, nor did we call them. We felt they were saying: 'Go back, it is not safe out today.' In any case, there did not seem much point in fighting those waves all day—we were not in that much of a hurry. We reefed again, turned about and headed not back to

■ *Zefka* at sea

■ Audierne, a delightful town with a small marina

■ The port of Le Palais, Belle Île is well protected—but watch the ferries

■ The attractive buildings alongside the quay at Le Palais

■ Jon, left, and John enjoying breakfast at La Fregate, Le Palais

■ *Zefka* at rest at St Martin, Île de Ré

■ In St Martin, the marina and harbour are right in the middle of the town

■ The way out to sea from St Martin

■ The busy town of Santander

■ The Santander yacht club may be plain on the outside, but it is elegant inside

■ To enter the port of Gijon, you need to pass the first bay, where there is a fine church and the yacht club

■ Cudillero, a pretty fishing village between Gijon and Ribadeo; a good refuge, no more, no less

■ The beautiful ria of Ribadeo—the town and bridge are just visible at the right hand side

■ The way out to sea from the excellent harbour in San Ciprian

■ The hills and little bay at the village of Bares in Ria del Barquero gave excellent shelter from the westerlies

■ The dilapidated waiting pontoon at La Coruña; you have to jump the gap to the main pontoon

■ One side of the marina at La Coruña is protected by the breakwater, and the other side by this old castle

■ The Torre de Hercules lighthouse, with a modern statue of Hercules in the foreground

■ La Coruña's elegant town hall in the Plaza Maria Pita

■ Water breaks over a rock five metres below the sea near Lage

■ The distant Islas de Bayona seen from Bayona

■ The magnificent castle is just behind the marina at Bayona

■ The church on the hill to the north of Viana do Castelo is a good landmark

■ Cascais is a good anchorage, but foreigners are not allowed in the new marina

■ The Torre de Belem stands guard at Lisbon

■ Lisbon's Praca do Comercio

■ One of Lisbon's many squares—they are all different

■ Approaching Cape St Vincent (Cabo de San Vicente) is a memorable moment

■ The stunning rocks and beaches of the western Algarve are there to be explored—best by dinghy

■ The lighthouse at Gibraltar is quite low, and the Rock towers above it

■ *Zefka* and crew enjoying the warmth of the Med

Viveiro, but instead into El Barquero where it was relatively calm. So much for the British weather forecast; the wind must have been at least a force six.

In the peace of El Barquero, with the sun shining, we now went exploring and found that there was no room for yachts in the small fishing harbour. It is a rectangular basin in which mostly small boats are moored on lines from the sea walls. Opposite the harbour, the ria turns sharply to the west before dog legging back inland where it becomes very shallow. After we had inspected the harbour, I went below for a quick piece of toast—a somewhat delayed breakfast. I had never been keen on setting off before breakfast except when starting very early indeed—I know some sailors love to do so—and after this I didn't fancy repeating the experience!

Three anchorages are shown on the chart, and all are on the west coast. Because the wind was still howling from the west, we chose the little bay just inside the ria as hardly any swell was coming in. The wind was coming across a saddleback in the hills, just to the south of some moored boats, so we found a spot that seemed to be far enough from the rocky shore on the flank of the bay, and anchored there at the south end. The wind was still very strong and, as it came over the hill, it made the boat veer around through about 45 degrees. A strong wind continued to blow all day so we stayed on board, moving the boat to a slightly quieter spot in the early evening. Once we anchored there, *Zefka* lay still, so we had a quiet night. As the wind continued to blow hard, we wondered how *Wild Goose* had fared.

30th June: What a difference a day makes! The sun shone, the wind and sea were benign—and at last we made La Coruña!

We had intended to stop in one of the rias on the way, but now decided to go directly to La Coruña because it was less than 50 miles from El Barquero. La Coruña seemed to be eluding us, and no doubt many others who had told us that La Coruña was to be the next major landmark in their cruise. Would we get there in June? At about half past eight we weighed anchor beneath a grey sky, and soon afterwards raised the mainsail.

The Leisurely Route to the Med

'Another grey Galician day,' I observed, as we headed gingerly out to sea. We had had no weather forecast whatsoever. Although there is supposed to be a station broadcasting weather information over the Navtex frequency in Galicia, *Mr Calico* had told us that it was 'dead'. It certainly seemed to be so.

When we emerged from the ria not only was there no wind, but no swell to talk of either. What a difference a day makes! There was hardly any wind worth talking about all morning, and what there was came from the west, not ideal. We motored quietly past the dreaded Punto de la Estaca de Bares, about a mile out to sea, and were pleased to see that the current was helping us, giving us an extra knot.

That headland is certainly a forbidding place, with reefs that extend some way out to the north-west, and a large lighthouse on top of the cliff. Spanish lighthouses are quite different from French ones, but are equally grand. Those on the north and west coasts are almost always perched on, or near, the top of a cliff so they do not need to be very high; in fact, according to the charts, they are frequently obscured by fog or low cloud that hangs on the headlands. The towers themselves are rather squat and usually at one end of a long and low building, presumably providing living accommodation. The buildings look as if they are big enough for the men and their extended families as well, which is just as it should be. We were to find that, generally, Portuguese lighthouses were similar.

Not long after Estaca de Bares is Cape Ortegal, another headland deserving of a wide berth. After those imposing headlands, the coast is less rugged and more beautiful. There is a mixture of steep cliffs and hills covered in rich green foliage that slope right down to the sea. Just before lunch we passed the entrance to Ria de Cedeira, which looks a very attractive little ria, and as the wind was freshening slightly we raised the foresail. The entrance is quite narrow with a marker buoy on a rock right in the middle, so it is necessary to go far to the west when entering. The ria itself bends round to the east. There are two nice beaches and a tall lighthouse on the western side of the entrance. Miraculously, the cloud dispersed as we passed the ria and from then on we enjoyed a nice sunny day—no engine, just the satisfying sound of the hull moving through the water. The wind had turned around to the north-west. Peace reigned.

Excitement off the north coast

Once we were off Cabo Priorina we could just see a city ahead in the haze, and then two towers in the distance. One is the Torre de Hercules, the lighthouse of La Coruña that has been operating continuously since the second century AD. An amazing piece of nautical history. The other is the modern control tower for the port. When you approach from the north east as we did, Torre de Hercules is not of navigational significance because it is well to the west of the port. The landmark we needed was the new control tower. It is at the root of the main breakwater and about as tall as Torre de Hercules, but white apart from the actual control room near the top.

La Coruña is in the south arm of a large ria. In the north arm is the city of El Ferrol, which has a military port. In the middle body of the ria are a couple of villages, Sada and Fontan where there is a marina. However, we needed to go into La Coruña to buy more gas and some food.

When we were about five miles off, we heard *Wild Goose* calling up first one marina and then another on the VHF, and were glad to learn that they had got to La Coruña safely. Their efforts to raise anyone seemed to be in vain and reminded us what an Englishman, who lives in the south of Spain, had said:

'Forget about calling marinas on the VHF. In Spain everyone uses a mobile, don't they?'

We have since found that some marinas do listen on channel 9, but none on channel 16. We took that advice and used the mobile to phone the Real Club Nautico, which operates most of the moorings in La Coruña. The phone numbers of marinas and yacht clubs are included in most pilot books. When they found someone who spoke English, the answer came:

'Yes, we have some spaces available. When you come into the marina go to the waiting pontoon which is at the end of the first pontoon. Then come to the office.'

I thanked her and we headed in. We passed through a maze of yachts moored on buoys and thought how easy it would be to pick one up, but we wanted the convenience of a pontoon mooring. We circled around, finding our bearings. If you approach along the channel inside the breakwater, as we had done, the waiting pontoon is at the end of the fourth pontoon, not the first, but because it has a sign 'Waiting Pontoon' it is easy to find.

In front of this sign was a wooden raft about 20 feet square, partially submerged. We motored past, assessing the situation; it looked most uninviting. Not only was it lop-sided and very short, but it had huge wooden cleats each at least two feet long, and one of them was partly under water. There was also a gap between this raft and the end of the pontoon of about two foot six! Even so, it was easy enough to tie up to the waiting pontoon for a short stay. But that was not the end of the surprises. There were no finger pontoons in the marina! We would have to go bow into the main pontoon and pick up the submerged mooring line, which holds the bow off the pontoon. We had not expected to find this type of mooring until we reached the Med.

I jumped the gap and went to the office where they found me a *marinero* (marina assistant) who would help us moor. This is pretty normal in Spain. I explained that this was our first experience of these mooring lines so would he please help. He nodded. We went around and headed straight into the pontoon—we were right at the end—and he was waiting to take the bow when we got close. Pauline passed him a rope which he tied off at a cleat, and then, grasping the mooring line, which is tied at one end to the pontoon, he jumped aboard and lifted the line out of the water as he walked along the deck. When he arrived at the stern, he pulled on the line, thus pulling the boat back from the pontoon, and tied it off really tightly onto the port stern cleat. Meanwhile Pauline had tied off the other bow line, and that was that. Actually, not as difficult as we had anticipated, particularly if there is someone on the pontoon. Once you get used to this method of mooring, it is fine so long as there is little rise and fall of the tide—as in the Med. We had no problems at La Coruña but in some ports, where there is a tide of two metres or more with fixed pontoons, this method of mooring makes it difficult to keep the bow of the boat close enough to get on and off easily, without getting too close when the tide falls.

Chapter Eight

A break in La Coruña

AT LAST, we had made it to La Coruña, a voyage of 900 miles, some of which had been easy, some exhilarating, and some challenging. We had not worked it out at the time, but we were more than halfway to the Med, and had spent just over three weeks getting there. As we looked around the pontoons, and up to the large building of the yacht club, we smiled with relief and some satisfaction. Now, we felt in need of a break, and there were chores to be done, but we also felt keen to get on. We were really having fun! We went up to the bar on the top floor of the yacht club and had some wine and olives, looking out at the gorgeous view across the marina to the ria and enjoying the lovely warm evening. It was a happy moment.

We spent a couple of days in La Coruña ; the first was intended but on the second we awoke to strong winds and so decided to stay. The city is interesting and attractive, and the people friendly. Although the marina

The Leisurely Route to the Med

has all the facilities you expect and staff are helpful, everything is a little old and rundown. One absurdity is that, although reception is manned from 8am-9pm, the showers and toilets don't open till 9am, and are locked up again at 9pm. Also, the water supply to the pontoons was turned off at 10pm each day.

Our time there gave us the chance to meet the crew of *Wild Goose* again—and of some other boats, too. *Wild Goose* had had a terrible day when they left Viveiro, realising as soon as they passed the headland that the sea was too rough for the boat. But they pressed on and after a 12-hour slog they had covered only 30 miles, and sought shelter in the Ria de Cedeira. The skipper told us later that he had done several Fastnets, but in larger boats, so he was obviously used to bad weather. That day's heavy sailing coming so soon after the crossing from Ireland had been too much for the third member of the crew—he had promptly jumped ship and headed back home.

The two men remaining on *Wild Goose* were taking her to Almeria for the skipper's sister. She had married a Spaniard and was now living there. Because the skipper had to get a flight back to London for a wedding, he had been hurrying. The other man was a dinghy sailor, and a qualified instructor, but had hardly any experience of sailing yachts. It was the instructor who was to be left with the boat, which needed a little work doing to it following the rough weather she had experienced, while the skipper flew back to London. He was due to return to complete the voyage; of course, that had to be finished in time for him to fly back to Cowes for the Fastnet in August! We know that *Wild Goose* did get to Almeria because we saw her sitting comfortably in the yacht club marina the following winter.

While we were shopping, *Holly*, a Nicholson 32 we had seen moored in Viveiro, arrived. They had spent a night on the anchor in the ria before coming in. The boat was crewed by a couple of retired men. One was now heading home, and the owner was staying in the port until his daughter and partner arrived for some cruising in the rias. They had had an uncomfortable crossing of the Bay of Biscay in rough weather, and spent much of the time with hardly any sail up and the boat under the control of the wind-vane steering gear. As one of them remarked:

A break in La Coruña

'We spent the time where any civilised people would—down below on our berths.'

While in La Coruña we had a chance to ponder about the bow-to moorings and look at how others solved the problem. Because you can moor close to the low pontoons there, you really need a short ladder rather than a passarelle. We found a neat one on a German-registered 43-footer opposite. Actually, the skipper was German but his wife was English. Attached to the support for the bow roller was a short ladder with three steps. It had a forked arm that supported the bottom end on the bow. When we remarked how neat it was, the skipper said:

'It is actually a standard little ladder I bought in Holland. I modified it to fit on the bow, and it works very well.'

His wife told us that they were heading for the Mediterranean, and asked us where we were going next.

'I'm not sure,' I replied. 'We will probably stay in one of the rias next.'

'We're going on to Camarinas,' she said. Camarinas is quite a large ria in which there is a marina.

'Yes, I expect we will be heading for that one,' I said.

She asked where we had come from, and we told her. Up to that point we were unsure of her nationality, but she asked:

'Can you detect my accent? I come from south of London, but I lived in South Africa for quite a long time, and now Germany.'

It seemed that they had been everywhere, and when Pauline asked about washing machines she replied:

'I think there is one here, but I don't really know because we have one of those small, hand washing machines. I find it works very well, and makes us more independent.'

I had heard of these little machines, and it was interesting to hear that they worked. In fact, there are two washing machines in the clubhouse, and you paid 580 pesetas to use one. I took a load of washing in and chose the hot rather than the cold wash. Technical stuff, this washing; I knew that we didn't want a cold wash, but did not take much notice of the fact that the hot temperature was 60 degrees C instead of the 40 degrees we

The Leisurely Route to the Med

use at home. That was a mistake! My new sailing trousers were now a mass of creases and all the whites were pale blue, and not a blue we would choose.

We found that we could get Camping Gaz at a small chandler just past the Hotel Finiseterre. Like most Continental chandlers it stocks only a few necessities and clothes, but not the extensive range of products you see in British chandlers. They did have the gas, though, and it costs much less than in the UK.

Later we walked along the new Paseo Maritimo past the docks to the city centre, which took about 10 minutes. The Paseo has been refurbished very well, with wide pavements and large beds of shrubs, and some ingenious rubbish bins that look like ventilation shafts on ships—they are vertical cylinders which turn horizontal at the top, and end in bellmouths. Very discreet and neat.

The balconies of the upper storeys of most of the old buildings that look out over the port are all glassed in, and hence La Coruña has been called the city of glass. More memorable, however, is the beautiful Plaza de Maria Pita, a wide, open square. Near the middle, facing the magnificent town hall is the statue of Maria Pita. Otherwise, there is nothing in the square to detract from the elegance of the buildings, which are all in the same style, with cloisters to give shade from the midday sun, and balconies above. This is surely the archetypal Spanish plaza, and none the worse for that. A good place to have lunch, and there are plenty of restaurants to choose from.

A remarkable feature of La Coruña is that part of the city is on a small peninsula—and the Torre de Hercules is sited at the seaward end. On the Atlantic side is the Bay of Orzan, which is circular with a lovely golden beach. It was quite near there that we found a really excellent vegetarian restaurant, Bania, which is on Calle Cordelaria. In fact, it is the best vegetarian restaurant we have found in Spain, with the excellent food matching the stylish décor. One of the nice features of La Coruña is that there is a maze of narrow alleys, closed to traffic, behind the port. There are plenty of good bars and restaurants and shops in this area which is very popular.

Unfortunately, the marina is nowhere near any restaurants or shops, and the nearest supermarket, which is underneath the market, is a fair walk away. There are many fine buildings in the business part of the city,

A break in La Coruña

including imposing edifices occupied by all the big local banks; now we are entering the internet age, these must be obsolescent Neanderthals, and are unlikely to be used as bank buildings in ten years' time.

We were held up for only one day at La Coruña, but it is the sort of place which we could have enjoyed had we been holed up there for a week, as we heard some people were. We did have time to walk up to the Torre de Hercules and marvelled that it had been there, looking toward the Americas for so long.

Although a weather forecast was posted daily in the club, it did not arrive very early so we had to use the outlook from the forecast of the day before when we were planning to leave. We were still in no-man's land, as far as weather forecasts were concerned, and would remain so until we were able to pick up the forecasts broadcast from Finisterre, which would not be for another day or so. We were all set to leave by half past eight the following morning, and even had the engine running, when another amazing incident took place. Pauline was on deck, and she said afterwards:

'I was just making sure that the bow lines were free to release when I became aware of a French yacht heading toward us still under sail. At first, I thought they were heading for the waiting pontoon nearby, and stopped what I was doing to watch. I have heard about people who spurn the use of their engine preferring to practice their skills at mooring under sail, but it became apparent very quickly that these men were not in that category. They were heading straight for us at some speed!'

'They came alongside still sporting some sail, when a man, dressed in full foul weather gear and wellies, leapt from the bow of their boat onto *Zefka* shouting:

'We have no engine since ten hours!'

'Then there was a thud as their bow hit the pontoon. I think at that point the skipper released the sail. Hearing the commotion, John came up on deck thinking dark thoughts until the skipper explained the situation again.'

We helped them tie up to *Zefka*—as they were right on the end of the pontoon there was no space for them to moor where they were. The skipper apologised:

'We thought your boat looked strong. We could not get onto the waiting pontoon.'

They had done no damage to *Zefka*, and as soon as we heard that they had been beating across the Bay of Biscay for ten hours we sympathised with them, even though it had been a bit of a shock to the system at that time of the morning. Our neighbour was less forgiving.

'Typical French panache—coming in far too fast,' he commented disgustedly. Meanwhile we did wonder whether it was a coincidence that the two boats that had used *Zefka* as their brakes were both French.

The *marinero* was actually doing his rounds and we had already told him we were leaving so almost immediately he came and towed the yacht into a vacant berth further down the pontoon. With that incident over, we could set sail.

Chapter Nine

La Coruña to Bayona

3rd July: Fanfares when we left, fog banks, and a delightful anchorage as the wind freshened

AS WE slipped our mooring, three American frigates came round the breakwater heading for the port, with all crews on deck in white uniforms and their bands playing—quite a spectacle. We were leaving at the beginning of a regatta. As soon as we emerged from the protection of the ria we found ourselves heading into a swell again. We were now on the west coast, and from here until we turned alongside the Algarve on the south of Portugal the swell was to be a major factor in sailing. Indeed, the weather forecasts always indicate the expected swell, and it is usually expected to be one to two metres. The normal pattern is that it starts off at about one metre in the morning, and increases during the day. The prevailing direction of the swell is from the north-west, so it is not a problem—the boat just rides up and down it.

The Leisurely Route to the Med

There was already well over a metre of swell, and once we turned around the headland where the Torre de Hercules lives, we were driving into the wind as well. We were now heading almost west, so the wind was not following the normal pattern of prevailing northerlies. So what was new? We were still in Galicia, and still had to round Cape Finisterre, which seems to have more than its fair share of storms, so we were proceeding with optimism tinged with a little caution.

We motor-sailed on, but headed well out from the land to avoid a number of shoals, and so did not make good progress for some time. We had not been at sea long before it started to rain finely—this was the first rain we had experienced, when sailing, since Fowey. From La Coruña there is a long, gently curving bay to the first landmark—the Islas de Sisargas, which we could just make out in the distance as a dark rectangular mass rising out of the sea and almost connected to the mainland. A little later on we were able to switch the engine off but were sailing at only four to five knots. Almost immediately we entered a fog bank. At first, the fog was very thin, we could still see the distant lighthouse on the outer Isla de Sisargas, and visibility was not too bad. Then it thickened, so we started the engine so we would be ready to make a quick manoeuvre should we meet another vessel.

Fortunately, we didn't. Earlier we had seen a large yacht in front of us, which had hugged the coast on leaving La Coruña, but we lost that in the fog. Before long we passed out of the fog, and could now see the Islas de Sisargas like a stark, sinister fortress. Along part of the base of the outer island is a bed of small jagged rocks, almost like the first line of defence against marauders. The swell beats against these rocks, sending waves and spray flying ceaselessly upward. The north face of the island is almost vertical, while the top surface is flat, and surmounted by a lighthouse which looks like the castle of the evil lord.

As we passed Sisargas, at about three o' clock, we turned south-west expecting to be able to sail; but guess what? The wind now went around from west to south-west, so we needed to tack out to sea. Soon afterwards we entered another fog bank but that was, fortunately, thin and quite short. We were grateful to the GPS navigation system which had helped us ensure that we were sailing well clear of the rocks.

The rias of Galicia and on to Bayona

We had decided to anchor in the Ria de Corme y Lage, which has a fairly wide entrance from which one leg of the ria extends north to the village of Corme, and the southern leg extends not so far down to the village of Lage. With the wind coming from the south-west, Lage would be more protected than Corme.

There is quite a remarkable shallow just off the coast near the entrance to the ria. The general depth is 30-40 metres, but there is a small area where the water is only 5.7 metres deep at low water; a rock like a tall, narrow mountain must rise out of the sea bed, forcing the water upward. There is always white froth over this shallow, but every time a wave comes the water shoots up, sometimes three or four metres into the air providing a cascade of spray. An amazing sight, enough to make you think that some bad-tempered hobgoblins live down below.

By now the wind was blowing at a force four, and so we sailed into the ria quite briskly heading for Lage. There is a substantial breakwater on the outer side of the harbour, and it certainly looked large for a small place. As we passed it we saw, to our amazement, a large cargo vessel occupying the whole length of the main jetty. We had thought it was a small fishing village, and all the other vessels appeared to be fishing boats. To the south of the harbour was a long sandy beach, with a row of buoys to reserve the area for swimmers.

A large black schooner flying the French flag and called *Oiseau de Paradis* was anchored near the harbour, and a small yellow yacht—actually about 28 feet, but it looked very small—anchored well out. It was from Denmark. We anchored between the two and were well off the shore in about six metres of water in a lovely quiet bay with green hills inland. We were glad to find good shelter.

We awoke the next morning to hear a forecast of force four to five and rain. Yes, we were now near enough to Finisterre to receive their forecasts! When we looked out, it was raining and seemed more like a force six, so we decided to wait awhile and see if the weather changed. It did, but for the worse; during the afternoon the wind strengthened, and *Zefka* veered around as the wind and current fought for control. Both the other yachts remained as well.

We spent the day on the boat. It was quite wild out there, and a long way to row ashore. In any case, we just felt lazy. Time passed happily on the anchor—reading, sleeping, cooking and doing some planning. Later in the day the whistle of the wind and patter of heavy rain gave way to the sounds of children playing on the beach. Sometime in the afternoon the sound of loud music being played close to our boat brought us up on deck. It was coming from a large pleasure cruiser taking its passengers for a trip round the ria. As it looped around our bay, and the music receded, we thought how soon their sea voyage would end and how lucky we were to have another month ahead of us—the weather would surely improve soon! By the early evening three more yachts had joined us in the shelter of the ria; one from the U.S.A. and two from Germany.

5th July: A surprisingly easy sail down and around Cape Finisterre

It was raining again, but this time the wind did not seem too bad. We delayed our preparations for a little while, and the showers blew over. I looked across at the little yellow Dane, and saw the skipper, who appeared to be sailing single-handed, making ready to sail. I signalled to him to see if he was going, and he nodded. He indicated he was travelling south, and I did likewise.

With the wind from the south-west we kept fairly close to the headland to keep in the calmer water as long as we could. Once we were out in the sea, the swell came at us as usual; over a metre high, from the west initially, but later from the north-west. Our course was not far off south-west, so for about an hour we motor-sailed to keep a little closer to the wind than we could have done sailing. We saw the Dane leave later, and he was obviously sailing. Without the assistance of the engine, he dropped back rapidly. We did not see him again.

It seemed a long time coming, but eventually the wind went around and we were able to sail almost due south, beating at quite a decent speed, riding up and down the waves. Now the swell was coming from behind and we expected it to stay that way for the rest of the Atlantic coast. Because the pitch of the waves is quite long, most of the time the swell does not create an uncomfortable motion.

The rias of Galicia and on to Bayona

We met a couple of boats coming the other way, and we soon became accustomed to the sight of a yacht in the distance disappearing below the waves as it went into the trough, just leaving its mast showing. Surprisingly, although the wind was behind them, both were motoring. One had a sail up, but it was sheeted in tightly so that it was unable to provide any drive. Of course, sailing downwind with a Bermudan rig does require quite a lot of concentration, and no doubt they decided that it was not worth the hassle particularly with the extra problem of sailing against the swell.

It was overcast most of the time, not what we had expected this far south in early July—another grey Galician day, of which we had now seen many—but we were still able to enjoy the beautiful hilly coastline. Just before the entrance to Camarinas is a rocky crag of an island with a tall lighthouse and behind it, on the mainland, is an army of wind generators. The Spaniards are certainly well ahead in the use of wind energy, not just in the north of the country, but also on the south around Tarifa.

In the afternoon, the wind increased as we were now expecting, and we reefed down two panels. The wind remained with us until after we had turned into the ria behind Cape Finisterre—so well known from the weather forecasts. It means the end of the world, and no doubt seemed so to people who had primitive boats. We were particularly alert as we approached, expecting the wind to increase off the headland. It is covered in foliage, and from the side is reminiscent of the Sphinx in shape, except that there are no paws. Instead, the front swoops down to the sea almost vertically. Along the saddleback, it is just possible to see a few houses facing the other way, and we assumed correctly that these were on the outskirts of the village of Finisterre. The cape is actually a thin spit of land that runs south from the mainland, protecting the bay behind it.

There was still the same swell running as we came down toward the south of the cape, and saw the solitary rock that stands a short way off, about half a mile to the north of the southern tip. To be on the safe side, we followed the advice in the pilot book and kept about a mile off the cape as we headed into the bay behind. We had covered almost 40 miles and it was a quarter to six. The bay inside the cape is just as beautiful as the seaward side, with green hills running down to the sea, and the village nestling in the north corner. The ria actually extends south of the entrance, and also well inland to an inlet to the village of Corcubion, where there is provision for yachts. However, it is quite a long way inland, so we decided to anchor somewhere near Finisterre.

As soon as we turned north on the inside of the cape, the sea became almost flat, with just a little swell sneaking round the corner. The village and harbour are about three miles up from the cape, and there is a single breakwater protecting the harbour, which is enclosed by the coast on the north side. There is room to anchor just outside the harbour, either to the south of the breakwater, which we thought might be subject to the swell, or just to the north of the harbour itself. However, just past the harbour is an outcrop of rocks, so we decided to anchor further across in the bay near a long curved beach. We saw a German catamaran called *Black Out* near the beach, and anchored in the same area in sand, quite a long way from the beach. The sea was fairly still, with just a gentle motion.

Passing Finisterre called for a celebration. We had rounded the most westerly point of Spain long associated—in our minds and those of many sailors—with storms. We were in a beautiful place, it was calm and quite warm. What's more, that day we had passed the 1,000 mile mark since leaving Plymouth. When we left a thousand miles seemed a huge distance in a yacht, but it had gone surprisingly quickly—and we'd had fun. Definitely time to open a good bottle of wine!

6th July: We pass more beautiful rias, the wind strengthens, and we find an uncharted buoy on the way into Bayona

We spent a quiet night, and of course, were ideally placed to hear the weather forecast from Finisterre. It was reasonable. Before leaving, we motored along the bay to take a look at an anchorage at Sardineiro, just around a headland and up a short creek. It looked a lovely little place, and would offer good protection against severe weather. Having seen it we turned about and threaded our way through the dozen or so little open boats, in which people were fishing, and headed out to sea again. Yet another overcast morning!

This time the sea was fairly calm and there was no wind at all to start with, so we motored all morning, heading for Bayona, which had been recommended as a lovely place to stop by several sailors. That day we

The rias of Galicia and on to Bayona

passed one of the most beautiful pieces of coastline we had seen. Along this coast the hills are rugged, but not very high, mostly separated from the sea by rough strips of flat rocky land. There are not many beaches, but a few attractive villages near the coast, and entrances to three rias on the way. We felt drawn into some, but really needed to press on if we were to reach the Med before the end of July.

In typical fashion, the wind strengthened in the afternoon and the sky cleared. By half past three we had taken a couple of reefs in both sails, and were riding the quite large waves at around seven knots, with the odd surge up to eight knots. As is usual the basic swell is quite high in the afternoon, but every so often some higher waves come along. They seem to come in threes.

As we were approaching the three islands that guard the entrance to the Ria del Vigo, a large cargo vessel, coming from the port of Vigo, emerged from behind them. We had thought that such large ships would use the main channel, but a glance at the chart showed that the north channel is also wide and deep.

As we stormed on in the strengthening wind the dark sandstone islands stood out strongly against the deep blue sea and the hazy hinterland. Just north of the islands we had reefed an extra panel in each sail, and were still surfing along at over six and a half knots in bright sunshine. Just great. By now, the waves were really quite big, which made it difficult to make out the small buoys, which were leaning over in the strong wind.

The entrance to the bay of Bayona is just south of the main channel into the Ria del Vigo, separated from it by a couple of low rocky islands, and we had to pass well offshore of these before turning in. The bay is L-shape, with the harbour concealed behind a headland.

As we passed the islands, all we knew was what we had seen on the charts and in the Seafile pilot book. Therefore we expected that, so long as we passed well clear of the islands, we would be able to head straight into the middle of the bay, and line up a couple of markers until we turned into the harbour. We started to turn in a little. With the wind on the northwest quarter pushing us forward at quite a rate of knots, we suddenly saw a distant yellow buoy ahead, apparently almost on the coast opposite. There were no other boats in sight to give us any clues.

Pauline took the helm while I studied the charts again. Nothing was shown. Not a thing. Puzzled, I fished out the binoculars and tried to focus on the buoy, as *Zefka* rode up and down the waves.

'It looks like a south cardinal buoy to me,' I told Pauline.

'It can't be,' she shouted in dismay. 'If we go to the south of that, we'll end up on the rocks.'

I refocused. Now that we were getting nearer I could distinctly see the two downward cones.

'It's definitely a south cardinal buoy,' I said. 'Don't worry about the gap. I can see that there is quite a bit of sea in front of the rocks.'

She was not too convinced, but changed course to keep *Zefka* to the seaward side of the buoy. As we neared it, we could see it was a long way from the shore. The relative positions of markers and land can be very deceptive when approaching from the sea. It really is a shock to find an important buoy that is on neither the chart nor in the pilot book; that was the only occasion on the whole voyage that we did, I'm glad to say.

By now we had passed the two islands to port, and although there was still quite a swell, we had time to look around. It was absolutely beautiful; a sweeping sandy bay with hills behind and the little town of Bayona tucked in to the south. The sea and sky were deep blue and the distant islands shimmered in the sun.

Sitting on the headland like a crown is the magnificent low walled castle that used to guard the town. The headland is wooded, and the green trees set off the castle well; we were full of anticipation. However, we still had a little further to go before we could turn into the wind to lower the sails, and head into the harbour.

Once we turned behind the headland the sea was calm, and we could see the marina just below the battlements, but could not see much in the way of spaces, so Pauline called them on the mobile to enquire. She was told that if we went to the refuelling pontoon the *marinero* would find us a berth. That was handy; we needed some fuel.

As we circled about looking for the way in, we could see a replica of an old sailing ship, which we later discovered was modelled on the ship in which Christopher Columbus returned to Spain; not the *Santa Maria*,

The rias of Galicia and on to Bayona

which was abandoned on a sandbank, but the *Niña*. Bayona is where Columbus arrived on his return, before heading south to Lisbon and Cadiz. What a day that must have been!

We followed the instructions on how to reach the refuelling berth, and appeared to be heading for a mass of boats and a beach, whereas no doubt Columbus could go where he pleased! But sure enough, once we had threaded our way through half a dozen moored boats we could see the large, empty refuelling pontoon ahead. When we stopped, we suddenly realised that it was hot; very hot.

What had started as a grey day 12 hours and 55 miles earlier was now a really hot day—and it was already nearly seven o' clock. This was more like it, this was why we were travelling south! Pauline realised later that while we were refuelling she had got covered in insect bites—the first of the voyage and probably the worst. The *marinero* showed us where to moor—another bow-on pontoon with a mooring line as at La Coruña — and he took the line as we came in so it was easy enough. We were next to a large American registered yacht, which seemed to be spending a long stay in Bayona.

We found that the marina was excellently run, with good facilities, although once again they did insist on locking up the showers from 8.30pm to 8am; needless to say by the time we went up for a shower that evening we were too late! The office of the marina and the other facilities were in an arcade below a restaurant, a lovely stone building with wide verandahs. At the far end the arcade opened out to the car park, a small walled garden and the gatehouse with a guard to maintain security. All the buildings are made from the same stone as the gate and walls of the *parador*, which used to be the castle. A *parador* is an expensive hotel set up by the Spanish government, initially to overcome the lack of accommodation for travellers.

The next day was the day before Pauline's birthday. We decided to start celebrating then as the following day we would be sailing and so have less opportunity for eating out. Bayona is a pleasant little town, with many attractive little alleys filled with restaurants, and several small supermarkets. The marina is close to the town and a few small beaches.

The Leisurely Route to the Med

After stocking up with food and lots of mineral water in the town, we headed for the elegant restaurant of the yacht club in search of a pre-birthday lunch.

From our table on the covered verandah we could see across the marina to the bay and hills beyond. It was a hot cloudless day with a light breeze cooling us. As we studied the menu some businessmen were enjoying seafood lunches at the tables nearby. Our choice was limited and the waiter was a little surprised when we ordered mixed salads, *Pimentos en Padron* and bread followed by a special Galician almond tart—and wine, of course. However, the food was very good. The pimentos were very small green peppers fried with chilli in olive oil—delicious with lots of crusty bread, and a speciality of the region like the tart.

What with the sun beating down—it was now 29 degrees C—and the wine, it was time for a siesta. While heading back to the boat we saw an extraordinary sight: there was a cooker set down on the pontoon with its burners removed. It had obviously come from the large American yacht, *Snowflake*, and the owner was hosing it down! Presumably he was trying to remove the accumulated mess from their Atlantic crossing.

'A typical man's solution for dealing with an otherwise dirty job,' observed Pauline. But we couldn't see if it worked.

We met a delightful couple from a 35-foot yacht called *Kutani* at Bayona. They had sailed down from Devon like us, and kept their boat at Newton Ferrers, where they also lived. They had had a mixed trip down, being delayed a week in Camaret, five days somewhere on the north coast and four days at La Coruña.

'We know our boat is very seaworthy,' confessed Mrs *Kutani*, 'but sometimes the crew is not as good at handling the rough weather.'

We agreed with that. They were not in a hurry but were at a point where they needed to make the big decision: were they to go further, or return to Devon? They had already travelled some distance with the swell, and realised that if they were to turn back, they would need to do so now or face some rough seas for much of the voyage.

We had told them that we were on our way to the Med, and Mr *Kutani* explained that they were keen to get down there so that they could sail in the sun instead of around the English coast.

The rias of Galicia and on to Bayona

'But on the other hand, we are really enjoying our retirement in Devon, and if we keep the boat down further south we will miss all the activities of the yacht club,' he said.

Mrs *Kutani* added:

'And we don't want to lose touch with the grandchildren,' echoing a remark to be made by several other couples we met on the voyage.

We saw them the following morning, and bad farewell as we headed off to Portugal and Viana do Castelo, a short hop of about 32 miles, now recharged by our stay at Bayona. We did not see them again.

Chapter Ten

Bayona to the peninsula of Peniche

8th July: A lazy, hazy, almost windless day for the short cruise from Spain to Portugal

IT WAS a still, sunny morning as we motored out of the marina and, ever the optimists, we raised the sails just outside the sea wall. Although it was Pauline's birthday we had decided to press on, and no sooner were we on our way than the mobile phone rang; it was Pauline's elder daughter phoning to wish her a happy birthday. A good start. As we motored out past the battlements, we saw ahead a large black yacht that had been anchored at the opposite end of the bay.

Strangely, although there is a buoy to keep you from going too near the islands in the entrance to Bayona—which does not look strictly necessary, unless the visibility is very odd there at times—there are no buoys to help you keep off the rocks on the mainland. There is a lighthouse quite a distance inland from the low headland, but the shore between there and Bayona is rocky. Also, there is a reef that runs quite a distance out to sea from the headland, so a little care is required. However, in good visibility it is simple enough.

Once we were round the headland we struck out to sea a little, partly to give us a straight path to Viana do Castelo, and partly in the hope that there might be some wind there. As we did so we could see that the large black yacht was *Oiseau de Paradis*, which we had seen anchored at Lage. We were both motoring at a sedate five knots, and so for some time we kept a little behind them. There seemed to be no wind at all, the sea was smooth without any swell, and already it was 25 degrees.

By about noon, there was just enough wind to keep the sails filled, and of course, up to that time, our battened sails had just lain quietly and motionless—waiting for the wind. We were not too surprised that the unbattened sails of *Oiseau de Paradis* were tightly furled nor that the light breeze was pushing us ahead of them. Just as I was preparing some lunch, there was a flurry of wind that lasted for about 15 minutes and gave us an extra spurt of speed. Oiseau did raise a sail to catch it after about five minutes, but soon lowered it again.

The wind had died down to almost nothing as we passed the Spanish-Portuguese border, which runs down the middle of the very shallow river Minho. Just inside Portuguese territory, and right on the coast is a small fort; the first of many signs that the Portuguese went to great lengths to protect themselves in the old days.

Pauline continues:

'John made a good birthday lunch of olives, hot bread, hummus, salad and fruit. Shortly after lunch I filmed the mouth of the Rio Minho as we sailed into Portuguese waters. There was a small ceremony as the Spanish flag was lowered and replaced by the rather grand Portuguese one. A little cheer was heard—it was one more important land mark of our voyage and time to turn the clocks back to British Summer Time.'

As we had travelled south from Bayona, so the mountains had given way to hills, which are quite rounded. Unlike the mountains which rise straight out of the sea, these hills have gentle lower slopes that run down

Bayona to the peninsula of Peniche

to sand dunes and beaches. Just before we reached Viana we could see an old building on top of the hill that overlooks the town. It is a fine church, and a little further along is another grand old building.

Despite the absence of wind on the passage, about half an hour before we arrived at Viana do Costelo the wind sprung up. It was not helpful, because once we had turned into the entrance to the river that runs past the town, we were almost into the wind.

The entrance into the river is straightforward, although it is necessary to give the north breakwater a fairly wide berth. Once between the two breakwaters there is a series of 14 red and green buoys that direct you up the river to the marina which is on the port bank. When we entered the marina, we were fortunate in that the manager was on the pontoon—actually, we discovered later he was there because *Oiseau de Paradis* had just phoned. He directed us to an empty berth and we moored bow-to, picking up a stern line as at Bayona. *Oiseau de Paradis* followed us in a little later.

The mooring line was covered in mud, and the manager told us that this was because the marina had just been dredged; that was good news. I followed him up to the office to do the paperwork. It was a small part of a Portakabin, stifling in the heat with the temperature now over 30 degrees. He suggested that I should pay the following morning. The owner of *Oiseau de Paradis*, Olivier, a gentle, bearded Frenchman came into the office while the manager was producing my documents on the computer; everything seems to be processed by computer in Portugal, and many invoices bear the legend 'Processed by computer' in Portuguese should you be in doubt. Of course, the result of this fashion is that everything takes much longer than before.

Olivier told me that they were on their way to the Mediterranean, but were not in any hurry. His boat, which is 43 feet long, is unusual in that it has a drop keel. With the keel up, the draft is only 1.6m—the same as *Zefka*—but with it down the draft is no less than 2.6m.

When finished in the marina office, I had to repeat the whole process plus a few extras with the customs/police officer at the other end of the Portakabin. It does not do to enquire what happens to all that paperwork; we just hope they recycle all the paper. With the formalities over, we went

The Leisurely Route to the Med

off to have a shower; they were in another Portakabin, and according to the manager were temporary while the marina decided when and where to build something permanent. Don't hold your breath. Like the man said:

'It needs money.'

The showers and toilets were pretty awful, and the doors were jammed open to what I thought was just a field, but in fact turned out to be a track to the riverside. At least the flow of water was reasonable.

We had visited Viana in the previous winter and had so enjoyed the town that we felt we must stop there again. So, that evening we searched out the lovely little bar we had found previously. Viana is an old-established town and port in which most of the roads are still cobbled, and most of the buildings are old. There are a few alleyways between the main streets, and Bar O Manel is on a corner in an alley near the main street. Between that street and the river is a long, narrow park, where the trees on each side of the main path have been trained to make a tunnel; a cool place to walk in hot weather.

We knew that we would not find a vegetarian meal as such in Viana, so we had eaten some nuts before leaving the boat. We ordered salads, bread and a plate of chips with a bottle of the excellent local Vinho Verde—young wine, which is slightly fizzy; in this case it was a red wine, and only 9.5% proof. We had some really chewy, crusty bread made from unbleached flour, and the salads were large. Despite being new and therefore pretty lightweight the wine was very enjoyable. Needless to say we sat at a table outside in the alley, enjoying the warm evening.

Somehow, the Portuguese in many places we visited did not seem to be having a lot of fun, but Viana is different; people there were out enjoying themselves. There are plenty of cafés that stay open till late and sell a wide range of pastries and cakes which the Portuguese seem to love eating with their coffee. That might explain the rotundity of the older people. We followed the trend and sought out a coffee shop for the rest of our meal.

When we returned to the marina we had another moment of light relief. We saw someone who looked like an official entering the office and so asked him if he had a weather forecast. He did not say a word, but took us into the customs office where the officer was watching television. A few words were exchanged by the two men and the customs officer switched the television to the text pages and found the weather forecast. Not quite how we expected a marina office to present a weather forecast but this was Portugal! Anyway, the forecast seemed reasonable, so we decided to go on the next day.

9th July: Light winds, and another short run to Leixoes

We were all set to go, but there was no sign of the marina manager. When we found him, he decided to make a completely new form in the computer, which prolonged the agony. However, while I was waiting, I had a chat with the owner of *Shady Lady*, a 48 footer we had seen in the marina the previous evening. We had been amazed to see the crew all wearing heavy weather gear although the temperature had been over 30 degrees. All was explained when he told me that he and his crew of three had had to beat against a force six or seven for eight hours coming north from Lisbon.

The boat had been built in China under US management and now needed a major refit. He had bought it in Almerimar, and was taking it to England for the refit. Afterwards, they intended taking *Shady Lady* back to the Med.

'My wife and I had been cruising in a Nicholson 32 for years, and we decided that if we did not buy something bigger now, we never would. The Nick is a little too small for sailing with one's friends. Maybe all I'm doing is buying a big boat so my friends will enjoy it,' he said.

When I told him that we had met another Nick 32, *Holly*, in La Coruña, he said that he knew the boat and owner. Small world.

Our delay with the paperwork, which is one of the plagues of Portugal, was not important because we were heading for Leixoes, the port just before Oporto and only 31 miles away. We saw that *Oiseau de Paradis* had left by the time we were ready. It was hot again, but a little cooler than the previous day. There was a slight breeze in the morning, but we had to motor-sail, and were not able to switch the engine off until after lunch.

One benefit of the light winds was that there was hardly any swell, and we had a pleasant run down the coast. Leixoes is easy to find because it is just past an industrial complex, where there are several tall chimneys.

The Leisurely Route to the Med

The marina itself is inside the port, and entry is not as simple as it might be because there is an old breakwater outside the existing one just below water level. We followed the fishing boats in taking a wide line. There is a fishing port, commercial port, some naval wharves and the marina in the port, so once inside there is plenty of room to manoeuvre. At first we needed all the space we could find, however, because as we entered a tiny fishing boat was laying a net diagonally across the entrance!

Leixoes is a good marina, within its own harbour walls, friendly staff and good facilities. However, the downside is that because it is inside the port the water is dirty, and the decks of the boat get covered in dust from the chimneys of the factories up the road. The area behind the marina is rather scruffy with simple little houses where workers from the port must have lived for generations. It is therefore very ordinary for the most part. Perhaps to serve the executives in the factories, which seem to be chemical plants, there are some restaurants that look pretty good. We saw one amazing restaurant where all the tables were already laid up for dinner. The walls and tables were all dark brown, but the tables were laid with elaborate damask tablecloths, heavy cutlery and ornate coloured glasses. Just another world.

After shopping we wanted a drink, and found a bar inside the local baker's shop! Just inside the door was a semi-circular bar, and in the back of the shop was the conventional counter with bread on display. When we arrived a woman was cleaning the counter and we presumed that she would serve us. No way! She steadfastly continued wiping the counter down, and eventually the owner came from the other counter to serve us. She was obviously the cleaning lady. I had a coffee, Pauline had an orange juice, and we shared a dense chocolate cake while we stood enjoying the atmosphere as various locals came and went.

They were proud of their bread in that shop. On the walls were posters explaining how bread is made and why it is nutritious, and some French scenes showing bakers delivering or selling bread a hundred years or more ago. There was a good selection of bread on the shelves, but we had just bought a loaf in the general store so had to refrain from buying more. Interesting loaves do abound in Portugal; wholemeal, sour dough bread, bread made with unbleached flour and corn bread. The light airy loaves, prevalent in France and Spain, are also available. It was the Portuguese, a seafaring nation for hundreds of years, who took bread to Japan.

That evening Pauline met Olivier, the skipper of *Oiseau de Paradis*, who had arrived earlier, and he said he was looking for somewhere to winter in the south of Spain. She told him that I knew the Costa del Sol well, and that if he came along to the boat we could have a chat. Later he arrived with his pilot books.

'We are heading for the Mediterranean, but are taking our time,' he said. 'We are planning to spend five years in the Med and want to spend the winter in Spain. We are not so keen on Portugal because most of the boats here are small motor boats. There is not so much room for larger yachts like mine.'

Olivier said that they wanted to be near or in a town, but not too large. I recommended Estepona, Marbella—not Puerto Banus, as it is too expensive, not just for the mooring but all around—or Fuengirola, so long as they had completed the extra breakwater to prevent the swell from the Levante entering.

'Duquesa is also nice, but is some way from the town, which is small, so is not so good for a long stay,' I said.

I asked him where he was from, and Olivier said that they lived near La Rochelle. We said that we knew someone who lived in Spain who came from La Rochelle and she said that it rained nearly every day. Olivier nodded.

'In the winter, if it doesn't rain, it is almost raining, and you can hardly tell the difference. We get just the same weather there as you get in the south-west of England,' he said. 'Wet.'

'We were there in the winter one day, and it didn't rain, but it was very cold,' I said.

'Yes, it can be cold as well,' Olivier observed. 'Do you know, quite a few British people come over in the summer and enjoy the warm weather, and think it must be nice in the winter. Then they come to live near La Rochelle, sometimes with their boats, and are very disappointed in the winters. By the way, what are your plans?'

'We are heading for the Med, but need to get back by the 1st August or thereabouts, so we are not staying long anywhere,' I said.

'We want to get to the Med,' said Pauline, 'But we will be happy if we get to Lagos, and leave the boat there. Then, we will come down when we can—probably in the winter—to move it on a bit further.'

'Are you going into Oporto?' Olivier asked.

We both shook our heads and Pauline replied:

'We spent a day there in the winter and don't really have time now.'

'If you ever do, don't try to sail up the river to the town,' Olivier warned. 'It is best to stay here because since they built the barrage—I'm not sure what the word is in English—the path the water takes has changed, the sandbanks are much higher than they used to be and shift a lot. It is a pity, but it is now easy to run aground. We are staying here for three days so we can spend some time in the city, which we like very much. Are you going to Lisbon?'

'Oh yes,' I said. 'We plan to spend a few days there.'

'It is lovely, with a nice atmosphere. And do you know, every area has its own atmosphere, like different towns. You will enjoy it.'

Olivier returned to his boat to enjoy a few days in Oporto, while we planned our passage to Figuera da Foz.

10th July: Poor visibility, and a dull day except for excitement when mooring!

With a trip of over 60 miles ahead, we were up early and set off at half past six, having first been appalled at the amount of dirt that had accumulated on the decks in the night, and a little apprehensive about the poor visibility. The forecast had been for a north-westerly wind of force two to three, which should have been helpful, but in fact, we started with a south-westerly of one to two. As we were casting off our lines, we saw a boat entering the marina, and waited for it to pass; we were amazed to see that it was a yacht that had been in the marina the night before. They had gone out and come back. What did that mean? Was it really foggy out there? Had they just heard a dreadful forecast? With those sort of thoughts running through our minds we set off to find hardly any wind, a bit of a swell, and mist. Visibility was over a mile, so there did not seem any reason why we should not press on. We did not bother to put the foresail up, and just motored through the gloom. The mist dispersed after an hour or so, but visibility remained poor, and when the sun did appear it was visible through the cloud surrounded by a halo. Although the sun did not break through that day, the weather didn't change much either, except that by three o' clock we were able to sail.

We did not see the entrance to the river Douro at Oporto at all, and later we could see the coast, but not in detail, which was a shame. There were a few hills, but the coastline was mostly flat, with a lot of unspoiled sand duncs, and also some salt flats for many miles. Although the sailing was simple enough, the sea is just littered with fishermen's floats of pots requiring a minor detour almost every few hundred metres. The huge number of floats is quite a serious deterrent to sailing at night along the Portuguese coast unless you go a long way out.

At about one o' clock we passed the entrance to the River Aveiro, where there is a port and an anchorage. Visibility was so poor that we could not see anything of it from about three miles off, but we saw some large ships heading straight for the shore there. The south side of the river is industrial, but there is a small village on the north side where you can anchor. With a shoal draft boat this must be an interesting area to explore. However, there is a bar at the entrance, and the tidal currents are fierce—evidently up to eight knots normally, and a highly dangerous fifteen knots in the rainy season.

About halfway to Figuera da Foz we were visited by a school of dolphins. Most just swam alongside and dived under the boat a few times before carrying on their way, but four or five of them decided that *Zefka* was good fun, and stayed with us for a while. They leapt and dived, sometimes in front of the boat, sometimes alongside and sometimes behind—they are so fast that they can be behind the boat one moment, and in front of it the next. Some of the group were larger than the others, and we could hear them snort as they came out of the water to breathe. On these occasions, you really do feel that the dolphins want to make contact with you.

After some rather dull countryside and poor visibility, we eventually caught sight of some higher hills standing out against the grey sky. This was Cabo Mondego, which is not many miles from Figuera da Foz. Once we had rounded the cape we turned in a little toward the port, which we could barely see. Between the hills and the town are the beach, flats and hotels of the town, which has been a resort for about a hundred years.

A pair of breakwaters lead into the river at the town, and big blocks are piled up on the seaward side of both, as is common on this coast. The one to the north of the channel is seen clearly, but the one to the south looks just like an island as you approach. Figuera da Foz is not an easy port to enter, however. Indeed, when there is a strong westerly wind blowing, you are forbidden to enter or leave the port anywhere near low water—we met a couple who had been holed up for about four days as huge rollers came in between the breakwaters. They told us that the harbourmaster enforces the rule rigidly. A flag is flown on the old lighthouse to indicate when conditions are this bad, but would not be too easy to see from off the coast. Although we entered just before low water, the sea was fairly flat, and we had no problems crossing the bar.

We made our way up the river to the marina, noting that the Seafile talked of a tricky cross current at the entrance, which we assumed meant just outside. Just to complicate matters, a dredger was anchored in the river by the entrance, and there were buoys around it warning boats to keep clear. As we approached we could see that the dredger was just past the entrance, and so I turned in watching the current carefully. No problem.

We were just wondering which berth to take—there were plenty empty—when we saw someone on the pontoon pointing across to the far side of the marina. Opposite the entrance was a building on the quay with 'Recepcioa' written on it. A man was waiting there. So I changed course, and we moored there.

It turned out that this is not the marina reception, but that of the police/customs. The official came aboard while I filled in all the forms, and the man apologised for his English but said that he had chosen French instead of English at school.

'But now I need English more than French,' he said.

When the formalities were over he said we could go and find any mooring we liked, and that he would take a copy of the form to the marina office, a Portakabin at the far end of the marina. The marina at Figerua da Foz is long and narrow, with the entrance in the middle. Fishing boats moor one end, and the marina occupies the other half of the basin. It is arranged in English style with long finger pontoons and there was a double space between two fingers nearby which we headed for now, planning to moor alongside the starboard one. As we approached an English couple came from their yacht and ran to help us shouting, 'Aim for the port side!' The cross current was evidently not outside the marina but inside—right across our path! We were not quite prepared for its speed and strength, and as *Zefka* was moving very slowly forward, she was being carried sideways at a fair rate. The English couple had had the same experience and fended us off as we came alongside the pontoon. After we made fast they showed us a deep v-dent in the pontoon made by the previous occupant.

'When we came in we were aiming for the left-hand finger, and ended up alongside the right-hand one. The current just cuts across viciously,' said the man, whose boat *Eagle Moon*, a Moody 34 with a tall doghouse, was moored at the other end of the pontoon.

11th July: Fun and games getting out of the marina; a dull day with little wind as we discover the fascinating peninsula of Peniche

The current had not finished with us. The next morning we were off to Peniche, another 60-mile passage, and I was thinking that we might pull the stern across toward the other pontoon when Pauline had the idea of warping the whole boat across sideways to the other finger pontoon before we left. That would allow some room to manoeuvre before the current could take us across to our downstream neighbour, a 47-foot Dutch ketch with a dinghy hung astern on davits. So we needed to clear about 55 feet before we would be safe.

Naturally, the Dutch crew heartily approved of our tactics and hurried over to take our warps and give us the best chance. When going astern *Zefka's* prop-walk sends the stern quite sharply to starboard so we just had to go for it—with full throttle astern, the warps were thrown on deck. *Zefka* accelerated fast and slid past the Dutch yacht missing the dinghy by a foot or two. Phew! That was a close one.

I kept her going astern and did almost a full circle so that we were facing the mouth of the marina, much to the amazement of a man just leaving the other end of the marina in a small dinghy. Then, we motored straight out and off down the river.

The Leisurely Route to the Med

Once again the Navtex promised a northerly wind, this time of force three or four, but in fact we ran into a south-westerly wind of force one or two as we turned in to the sea to head south-west. The visibility was quite poor and remained so for another day. We had had a taste of hot sun but even this far south it was not guaranteed in July. And there was little wind, which tends to make me somewhat grumpy. We want to go sailing, after all! Some wind did come later, and swung around a little, but we still needed to keep the engine on.

There is a small marina and fishing port at Nazare, about 40 miles south of Figuera da Foz, but we wanted to go as far as we could to make up a bit of time. However, Nazare is a useful refuge. Further south is a most remarkable little harbour, which is a surprise when you first see it. There are cliffs along this part of the coast, and suddenly there is a gap in the cliffs which appears to be filled with tall buildings! In fact, the buildings are well back from the cliffs, but because they are the same height they look nearer than they are. The harbour is almost circular, and surrounded by beaches except in front of the cliffs. There is a very narrow entrance through the cliffs, as if a hole has been punched through them to give access. This is San Martinho de Porto, a very sheltered harbour. It is only about two metres deep, and evidently has a tendency to silt up. It would be a nice place to stop—so long as your boat has a shoal draft.

Further down the coast is another deceptive inlet into Lagoa de Obidas. It looks quite inviting from a distance but there is a sand bar and just a narrow, shallow channel, suitable for dinghies. Inland it widens out into a lake.

We motored on along the coast in fairly poor visibility until we could see what looked like a headland standing off from the land. As we neared we could see that this was not Peniche, but a pair of small islands which shelter the north of the peninsula—so we were not far away.

A little later we could see Peniche, which sticks out from the middle of the Portuguese coast like a knob, and by then the wind had died completely. The swell was still running, but there were no wavelets at all on the swell, so that in the strange light, with a little sunlight seeping through the clouds, the sea was like a dark desert.

According to the pilot you can anchor to the north of Peniche, but there is now a marina in the fishing harbour with a pontoon for visitors. We made our way round the end of the peninsular, and right at the end is a dramatic rock that sticks up out of the sea just separate from the mainland. Some say it looks like a woman with a child, and as we rounded the headland we had to agree; it was as if the woman was waist deep in the water, and carrying a baby in her arms.

From there on in, one would expect the course to be simple enough. Not a bit of it; fishermen's floats everywhere, right up to within 100 metres of the entrance and in the main fairway as well. However, the harbour entrance is wide, and the visitors' pontoon easy to find. You just moor beam on to the main pontoon that runs along the side of the marina. There were only two boats there, one British and the other Portuguese so we had plenty of room.

Chapter Eleven

More than we expected en route to Lisbon

THAT EVENING a middle-aged man came over from the British registered boat, a Beneteau 35, that was on the pontoon. The owner, a businesswoman, hired him and a friend to take it as far as Gibraltar with her. He told us that they had joined her at Penzance, sailed across to Audierne, and then directly across the Bay of Biscay in good weather. Round the north of Spain, they had encountered a force seven northerly wind, but had made rapid progress. Their last leg had been from the ria just to the north of Bayona to Peniche. He told us that he did not like Peniche because there was only one decent bar in the town, which was run by a professor of fishing.

'He speaks English,' he said, as if that explained everything.

Actually, we were to find several nice bars. We had decided that it was time for a day ashore as we were running short of provisions—the main problem was the need to buy bread, fruit and vegetables regularly. The next morning the other member of the crew of the Beneteau came over to talk to us, and said that *Zefka* looked a nice solid boat, and must ride the bad weather well. We said she did.

'Not like that,' he said, nodding towards the Beneteau. 'I couldn't even sleep last night, because it was moving about so much. The waves kept slapping the stern. It is quite quick, but it bounces about like a cork in any kind of sea.'

He also complained that he did not like helming, but that they could use the auto pilot only when the engine was running.

'On the passage down to Penzance she used the auto pilot when she was sailing, and ran the batteries flat, so she won't do that any more,' he said, clearly unhappy. 'We're going as far as Gibraltar, and then the owner is going back to the UK. She is sailing the boat down to the Canaries where she has taken a berth for six months, which seems a bit of a commitment to me. She wanted me to look after the boat while it was in Gibraltar, but I don't fancy a couple of weeks there,' he went on.

Off he went to continue their voyage—to Lagos, which his friend liked because of the beaches and big breakers where he could enjoy a swim. We went to the marina office, and found that the showers and toilets were small but quite good, and then headed into town. The street from the harbour into the town was lined with restaurants. Outside every one was a refrigerated glass case full of beautifully arranged dead fish, and a charcoal burner on which to cook them. As we walked we were bombarded with smells, many unpleasant. There was smoke hanging everywhere from the barbecues, cooking fish, rotting fish and drains. Despite this we still enjoyed the charm of a place which is really foreign and different. There was no doubt that we were now far from home. As is usual in most places on the Portuguese coast, there is not much variety in the restaurants. In Peniche, as in many other Portuguese seaside towns, the restaurants seem to specialise in barbecuing the fish on sticks. If you enjoy eating barbecued fish, Portugal is the place for you!

We did find plenty of bars serving pastries and coffee, and soon realised that Peniche was a favourite resort town with the Portuguese despite the gloomy weather. We may have been unlucky with the weather,

More than we expected en route to Lisbon

but when we mentioned it to the manager of a shop in Lisbon he told us that Peniche was a 'very cold place'—relative to Lisbon and not to London, of course.

One reason for its popularity is that there are some islands kept as nature reserves off the peninsula, and boats provide a regular service to them. Of course, the town, which used to be fortified with a wall all the way around, now depends mainly on fishing and tourists.

Back on the boat, we started to prepare lunch when a sudden rocking motion and the sound of outboard motors driven hard aroused our curiosity. There was a crowd of men waiting on the quay while about half a dozen open boats were racing flat out to pick up the men and ferry them to their large fishing boats, moored on buoys out in the harbour. The open boats made several trips delivering ten to twelve men to each fishing boat. Evidently those that were ready first and fastest got the most work in ferrying the crews across. Then, with their full complement of men, and a large dinghy hoisted up on the stern, the big wooden fishing vessels cast off and made for the open sea at full speed. Our boat and pontoon were tossed about by their wakes as about a dozen of these vessels left as if their lives depended on getting out by one-thirty. Were they all competing for the best fishing grounds—if so why didn't some leave earlier? They returned early the following morning, all within about twenty minutes, and the whole procedure was reversed. Quite a spectacle!

It was still cloudy in the afternoon as we went for a walk along the wall to the south of the town and then around the peninsula. To the north of the town were some very poor-looking hamlets with fields of sugar cane. By the coast the land was very barren and on the rocky coast we came across the remains of a fort. The peninsula is quite small so we had been almost all the way around and back to the town in an hour or so. It was a nice windy day—often happens when we decide to have a day in port.

That evening, we found a reasonable Chinese restaurant for dinner, and it was quite busy; even the Portuguese get fed up with fish now and again it seems.

The Leisurely Route to the Med

13th July: Windy—good, then better, then downright hairy

Now it was on to Lisbon, the third successive passage of 60 miles or so. We left at eight o' clock with a fresh northerly wind, reefed two panels while off the beach to the south of the town, and headed out to sea. Soon afterwards we needed to shake out a reef in each sail. It was still grey and cool, but good to be sailing from the outset. By lunch time the sun had broken through, and we were sailing along a beautiful coastline consisting mostly of sandstone hills and cliffs. With the blue skies came a stronger wind, and when the speed reached seven and a half to eight knots we took two reefs in dropping the speed by a knot, and continued to sail in the usual pattern of up and over and down the waves in the swell, now around two metres in height.

As we approached Cabo da Roca—about ten miles north of the approach to Lisbon—I heard someone calling us over the VHF radio. Eventually we made contact and it was a Spanish boat heading for Galicia—a long way to the north. They asked if we had any news of the weather. I read them the report we had received over the Navtex. It forecast a force four to five wind from the north with a swell of 1.5-2.0 metres, and that was what we were getting. They thanked us and said that this was 'useful information' no doubt because, like us they are used to fairly accurate weather forecasts. Their boat passed us a little later; it was motoring with only the mainsail up, and was heaving up and crashing down into the waves in such a way that it must have been horrendous on board. And at that time we did not know worse was yet to come.

All was well until we turned around Cabo Raso and headed south-east toward the wide mouth of the river Tejo and Lisbon. Fortunately the swell reduced a little as soon as we were past the headland, and we were settling in for a nice fast sail into Lisbon. I even wondered whether we might shake out a reef. As if to teach me for such an imprudent thought, the wind immediately strengthened, and we were earholing along at eight knots again with the wind almost directly on the beam.

'Reef!' called Pauline. 'The wind is too strong.'

I had to agree, so we took in one extra reef—just three panels up in each sail now. The boat sailed much better, more upright, but still hammering along through the light swell. Fine, I thought, and so it was

More than we expected en route to Lisbon

for an hour or so. But all the time the wind was getting stronger even though the sun was still shining brightly and there was hardly a cloud in the sky.

Before long it was obvious that we would need an extra reef, and the wind might strengthen further. We still had 15-20 miles to go to Lisbon, and we would soon turn into the main channel for quite a long beat up the river to the city. I decided it made more sense to head in to Cascais, where there is a large bay and well-known anchorage that would offer good shelter from the northerly winds. The Seafile said there was a new marina there.

Not long after I had taken that decision, we took in yet another reef, and so were down to just two panels—the triangle and one other panel. This was the first time we had sailed with just two panels, and *Zefka* was still sailing really well at six to seven knots. Her performance bore out the comment made by experienced junk-rig sailors, that these rigs sail very well when reefed right down. By now we were able to turn into the bay, and could see the long breakwater of the new marina, and wondered whether there would be any spaces available. The Seafile had indicated that there would not be spaces for visitors. We need not have troubled ourselves thinking about it; although the marina was supposed to have been finished in May, we could soon see that there was not even a pile in sight let alone a pontoon. Incidentally, we understand that now it is finished, visitors are not allowed to moor there because there is no police post on the port to process foreigners' documents.

Once in the bay in front of Cascais and Estoril, we let down the remaining sails and motored in. Local boats are moored on one side, and visitors anchor elsewhere. There was plenty of room and we anchored at about half past five after 48 miles. The wind continued to rage into the night, but the anchor held well. It was so wild that we did not undress that night and set the alarm for 2am to make sure all was well. By then, the wind had dropped a little. We heard the next day from the skipper of a boat we met in Lisbon that the wind had reached 35 knots when we were sailing. That's a force eight, which would have been serious had we been far out at sea. We felt for the crew of the Spanish boat heading for Galicia.

The Leisurely Route to the Med

14th July: A hot morning and a quiet run to Lisbon

As usual, there was little wind the next morning, but it was hot and sunny. We motored off, crossing the end of the sand bar, where the water is about eight metres deep, and entered the river Tejo. Arriving at Lisbon under our own power gave us enormous satisfaction. During the long approach up the wide Tejo we were feeling quite triumphant. A good seaworthy sailing yacht gives you the freedom to travel the world and, if you have time to wait for the wind, the power is all free! Many have done it and arrived at far more exotic places. But for us—previously short distance sailors—reaching Lisbon seemed a huge achievement.

We stopped for fuel at the second marina—Belem—which is just after the magnificent monument to Portuguese explorers. The fuelling pontoon is only about five metres long and is straight opposite the entrance, jammed between some pontoons. Well, we managed to get *Zefka* in and onto the pontoon without too much difficulty, but by the time we were ready to leave about half a dozen Optimists helmed by youngsters were milling around in the marina. They were evidently waiting for their instructor to join them. Meanwhile, there was one boat trying to get into a berth, and another waiting to refuel. We still found enough room to manoeuvre and leave the marina to continue upstream.

We already knew that Belem and the previous marina we had passed do not have space for visitors, and had been warned by Olivier that Santa Amara, the next marina, is very noisy because it is under the long road bridge that crosses the Tejo. The bridge carries the main road out of the city, and the roadways are actually made up of metal grids, so the noise comes straight down. We were astonished how noisy it was as we went beneath on our way to Alcantara, an old commercial basin in which there is now a marina—without finger pontoons but with mooring lines.

There was plenty of room, and we headed straight into an empty berth next to *Stryker*, a Halberg Rassy 35. The skipper took our bow line which made the job fairly easy. There were two men on board, and one had crewed down as far as here. Now 'his time was up' and he was ready to fly home. The owner's wife was due to fly in and take over crewing to Gibraltar, where they would meet her children for a cruise. So they would have to leave promptly in order to arrive in time. Meanwhile, we relaxed.

More than we expected en route to Lisbon

Lisbon was certainly an important milestone in our voyage, and now we were going to have a couple of days in the city, sightseeing. We had covered 1,347 miles according to the GPS, and it was five and a half weeks since we had left Plymouth.

Chapter Twelve

Sightseeing in Lisbon

ALCANTARA has some advantages, but when we were there the facilities were not among them. The showers and office were a long walk from the visitors' pontoons, and we were told that these were all temporary. They were pretty abysmal, particularly for a major city such as Lisbon. However, Alcantara is quieter than Santa Amara. Alcantara is also spacious, with plenty of room for big yachts, and there were some there. The railway station is just five minutes on foot, and five minutes further on is a large supermarket and a shopping area with a bank. It takes only about five minutes into the town on the train—a very cheap, frequent service—and one evening we walked back.

It was very hot the whole time we were in Lisbon, with the temperature over 30 degrees during the day, so we limited our sightseeing. We went to the Praca Comercal, a large square with elegant cloistered buildings on three sides, and the road that runs beside the river

The Leisurely Route to the Med

on the fourth. In the middle is a grand monument, and in the side opposite the river is a triumphal archway that connects to one of the old main streets, and thence to another square. In this street, which is closed to cars, are a number of banks, all of which have grand buildings; one even has its name written in the pavement outside.

There are several squares, each with its own atmosphere, quite close to the Praca Comercal and also nearby is the nineteenth century lift that was installed to take people from the main area of town to the Bairo Alto—high village—which is on the top of a steep hill. We walked up to that area and found older buildings on a more intimate scale, but still mainly commercial. There are a few streets that resemble Paris, and these are complete with outdoor bars where American tourists were holding forth to the world about their lives Stateside.

Our experience of these bars was of indifferent waiters who were not the slightest bit interested in serving anyone, and in this respect we found the centre of Lisbon unlike the rest of the country. They were not even willing to help an old lady who was distressed by the weather and the hill—and looked decidedly unwell. She was sitting on a chair but there was no available table so they refused to serve her. Having waited for service for quite some time, we gave her our table and went elsewhere. There, as at another bar the following day, we had to go up to the bar, where the waiters were hanging around, to ask for some service. This attitude seems to be peculiar to Lisbon, however.

We did find an excellent health food supermarket, with a good vegetarian/macrobiotic self-service restaurant in the basement; the supermarket is called Celeiro Dieta and is at Rua 1 de Dezembro 65, just 50 metres from the Praca Don Pedro IV. The restaurant is open for lunch only.

In theory, Lisbon has a good underground railway, but our experience was not good. We went just a couple of stations from the main station on one line, and then changed to another line to find that, owing to some major problem, it was out of action. So we ended up walking to our destination. It was then that we realised that the central area of Lisbon is quite small, and that you can walk round a lot of it—especially in the evenings when it is cool.

That evening we went to *Os Tibetanos*, a vegetarian restaurant recommended by one of the staff at the tourist office, where the interest in the customers was far removed from that adopted by waiters in central Lisbon. *Os Tibetanos* means the Tibetans, and the restaurant is in the Tibetan information centre at Rua do Salitre 117, near the main avenue in Lisbon, called simply La Avenida. It is the city's Champs Elysée, and very nice too, with avenues of trees and gardens beside the wide street. We were surprised to find that the restaurant was not only packed, but that people were queuing. So we waited, and were rewarded by an excellent meal with a nice bottle of wine—Porce de Murca from the Douro region.

In the morning, we went to change some travellers' cheques in the little bank in Alcantara, and it took about ten minutes and three people to do it. The bank clerk was a young woman who seemed to know exactly what she was doing, but the deal evidently required the active co-operation of two grey-haired men in dark suits. We thought that told us something of how things work in Portugal, which even the Portuguese admit is plagued with paperwork. Alcantara is a down-at-heel suburb of Lisbon, so we went there once only, but the Pingo Doce supermarket was surprisingly good. We also found a good bar/restaurant, which was evidently very popular with the locals, to judge from the number of places that were being laid for lunch. Service was good and friendly, which is generally what we found in Portugal.

Back at the marina, there were several restaurants in boats moored in the basin, and also a superbly restored ship. This was the last Portuguese sailing warship, and was rescued from a sandbank where it had been rotting quietly for many years. It is a three-masted square-rigger with about 40 guns poking through the sides; not a pretty sight if you happened to be an enemy, but now just an impressive relic. Would that all military equipment was similarly pensioned off.

Despite the inadequate facilities in the marina, we enjoyed our stay there. *Stryker* went off on the second morning heading for Lagos, and while we were out that day, *Magic Dragon of Herm*, a great name for a boat, arrived. She is an Oyster 55, and is no doubt a superb long-distance cruiser. Herm is the small island nearest Guernsey where *Magic Dragon* was registered. There were four people on board, a middle aged couple and

The Leisurely Route to the Med

a younger couple. The skipper told us that they had left Guernsey a year earlier to do more or less what we were doing, and were now heading back. They had spent too long beating up the coast fighting the swell, and were all exhausted, but hungry. Their recipe was to eat plenty of bacon sandwiches.

When we told them we were off to Lagos, the skipper opined:

'I wish we were going south. Heading north we'll have to fight the swell all the way up. Once you turn round Cabo da Vicente, the swell will disappear and the sun will continue to shine.'

Later Pauline observed:

'If we decide to take *Zefka* back to England I'm not sailing her against that swell and wind! We'll have to put her on a truck or go through the canals.'

While filling the water tanks and hosing the decks, in preparation for the next leg of the voyage, we forgot to close the portholes. It is just amazing how much water you get through a half open porthole when you aren't trying. Needless to say most of it went onto our berth, making a big puddle, so we had to put out all the bedding to dry off. Good job it was really hot.

Because our plan was to sail overnight to Lagos, we decided to put the radar reflector up. One minor disadvantage with a junk rig is that there is nowhere convenient to fix a Firdell Blipper permanently, so we use it only when necessary, hoisting it up and tensioning it with an extra cord. Anyway as I did so, the younger man on *Magic Dragon* thought he'd add a little ceremony to the occasion by imitating a bugle's salute as the reflector was raised, much to Pauline's amusement. Soon afterwards we slipped the mooring.

THE ROUTE:
La Caruña to Estepona

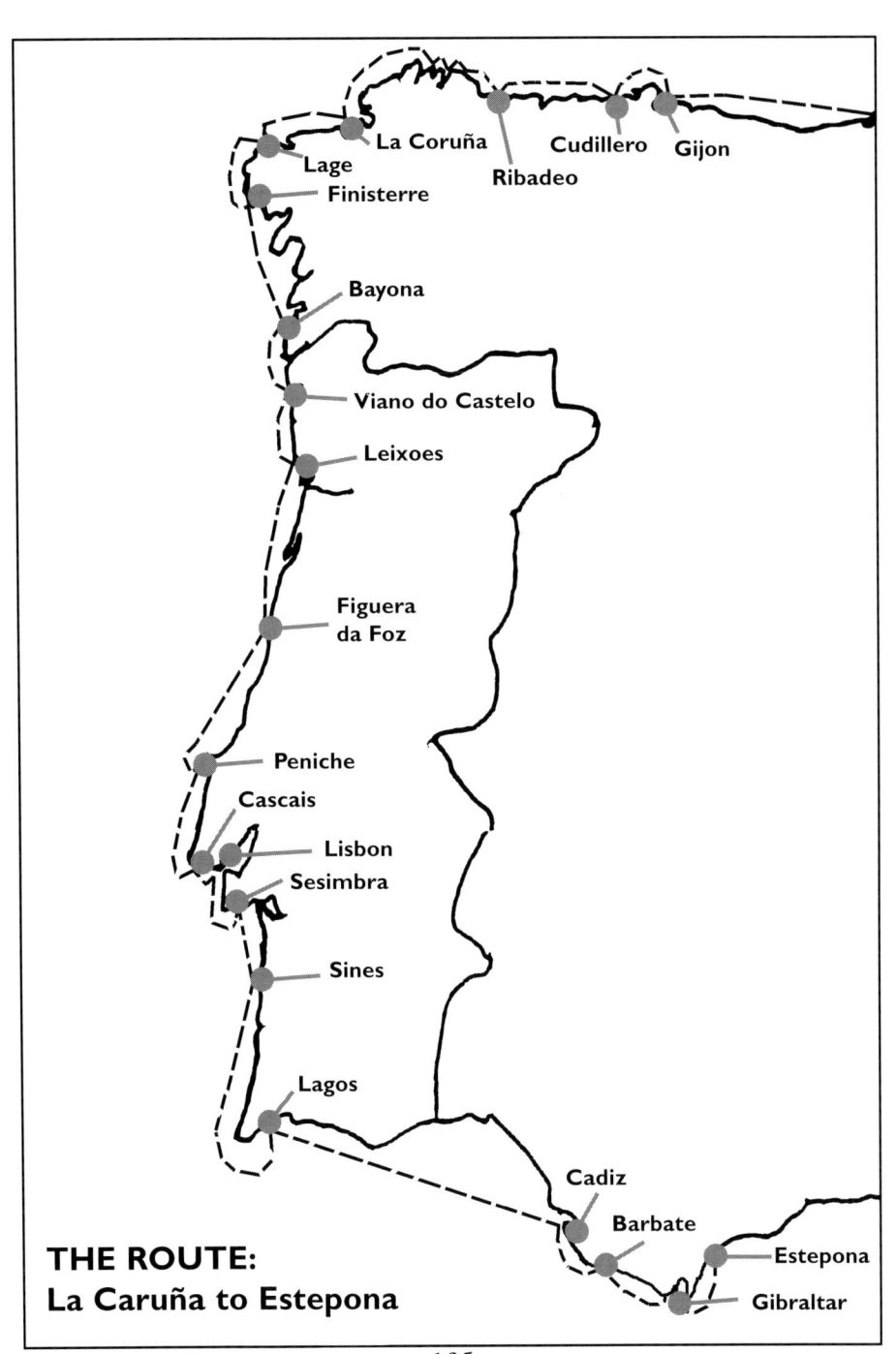

Chapter Thirteen

Lisbon to Lagos—in stages

17th July: The plan to go directly to Lagos scuppered by strong winds; another night on the anchor

WELL, it was only half past five that evening and we were riding on the anchor again. Our plan of sailing overnight to Lagos was literally blown away on the wind, and here we were in the shelter of the bay at Sesimbra, only 32 miles from Lisbon. We had put the sails up soon after passing under the bridge over the river Tejo, and there was already a good breeze. Since it was a Sunday morning, there were quite a few yachts out in the river and river mouth, including a large gaff-rigged yacht that was obviously taking people out for trips round the bay.

By the time the river was widening into the mouth, *Zefka* was flying along, heeling quite a bit and Pauline shouted through the wind:

'We need to reef. We're going too fast.'

The Leisurely Route to the Med

'I know,' I replied. 'But this may be a local effect. I want to wait till we're a bit further out to make sure that the wind doesn't drop off as soon as we clear the land.'

These sort of discussions were quite common on the voyage, and on this occasion we did hang on a bit longer, but in the end took in two reefs before we were completely clear of the land. Now turning south, but well off the coast, we continued to sail well. We overhauled another gaffer and noticed a couple of yachts keeping in close to the shore, which is mainly beaches and sand dunes for the first 20 miles or so.

Before long we had taken in another reef but, by one o' clock, the wind had dropped off and we had not only shaken out the reefs, but were also motor-sailing. That lasted for half an hour only. Then the wind came back with a vengeance. The swell was now large with lots of white horses. Here the coast runs down at a slight angle to Cabo Espichel then tucks in sharply for a few miles to a river entrance and the port of Setubal. We were heading for the cape.

Two hours later we had reefed down three panels in each sail and were just off the cape. We looked around for the other boats and at first they seemed to have disappeared. Then we saw the gaff rigger tucked in close to the cape, and heading towards Setubal, and another yacht heading in the same direction. Everyone seemed to be scuttling for cover.

As expected the conditions worsened as we approached Cabo Espichel. The waves were about two metres high and the wind was pressing us on at seven to eight knots. Half an hour later the spume was beginning to come off as spray so we guessed the wind was around a force six or seven. At that point we reefed again down to just two panels as we had going into Cascais, and the wind seemed at least as strong. Our experience indicated that if it was this windy in the afternoon, it was likely to be windier in the evening, and so clearly the idea of going to Lagos was not on. If we went as far as Sines we would arrive in darkness, which did not seem a good idea either, especially in that wind. So it had to be Setubal or Sesimbra.

We continued to race ahead and *Zefka* was riding along well. We took turns in studying the chart, and I thought shelter would not be good at Sesimbra—where we would need to anchor—and that it would be better in Setubal, even though we knew that the marina was small.

'Even if we anchor, we will be in the river, well out of the swell,' I said, but Pauline thought that Sesimbra would be quiet enough and it was a good deal nearer.

'Why don't we go and have a look'? she asked.

'OK,' I agreed. 'It is not far out of our way.'

Sesimbra is tucked into a corner, so we changed direction and headed towards the village. Once we had sailed for about a mile in from the headland the swell dropped appreciably, but the wind still swooped down over the land at quite a rate. We could now distinguish the different parts of Sesimbra. There is a fishing harbour, but they do not welcome yachts— except for a few permanent residents—so we looked for an anchorage. As usual at holiday resorts the long beach was cordoned off by a row of buoys to stop boats going too near the shore.

I did not like the look of the sea. Despite the high hills behind the town, the waves were larger than we had seen at Cascais. Nevertheless, the swell was not coming into the bay, so I decided to give it a try. We dropped anchor, put out plenty of chain and sat back to see what happened.

After 10 minutes the anchor was holding well, and although the wind was blowing up small waves they did not affect *Zefka*. She just sat there, bow into the wind. The strange thing was that, despite our concern about the weather, the sun was shining, it was a hot day and hundreds of people were out on the beach and in the sea. In fact, some people came quite near us on one of those pedaloes! Of course, the beach was completely sheltered from the wind, such a contrast from the conditions we had recently experienced.

One of the features of our Shipmate GPS is an anchor watch. You can pre-set the amount of drift you consider the safe limit and at that distance an alarm will sound. When we first tried it, the alarm kept going off when there were no signs that the boat had moved, it was just sheering around on the anchor. This time we set the distance at about 300 metres, which seems a lot but in practice a drift of that amount would not create any problems, and that way we would avoid it sounding too often. I also took bearings on a few landmarks so that I would have an extra check on our position. By either measure, *Zefka* hardly moved at all that night even

The Leisurely Route to the Med

though, late in the evening, the wind was howling more strongly than when we arrived. It blew all night, but when I checked our position at about 3am, all was well and we had a good night's sleep.

18th July: A sunny day with a good wind to take us on to Sines—now a long way down the coast

We decided to go on to Sines rather than Lagos, largely owing to the uncertainty about the weather. It was still windy when we weighed anchor, which took quite a while because it had really dug in. When it eventually came up there was a long streak of thick mud on one side where it had dug deep. I was pleased about that really because the anchor had now been well tested and shown to be up to the job. When we bought *Zefka* I thought the anchor was larger than we would need; certainly the 45lb CQR is much larger than one often sees on 32-34-footers, but I was now very glad to have it.

It was only just over 30 miles to Sines, so we did not leave early but waited to try to get a feel for the wind. We did not think it worth putting too much faith in the Portuguese weather forecasters; they had forecast Force 4-5 for the previous day, and were still doing so in the afternoon! In the sheltered bay it was difficult to judge the wind accurately, although it was obviously coming from the north, and we decided to sail with just three panels in each sail from the start. But after an hour we shook one reef out, and before long the wind had gone almost entirely!

Just to keep us on our toes the wind rose again, but not as it did the day before. It had swung around to the west, so it was on the beam and by lunchtime we were back with two panels reefed, and the swell was increasing. An hour later, we reefed an extra panel, and soon afterwards we were visited by a group of dolphins. As before, they played around the boat for about five minutes swimming fast alongside, diving below the bow and leaping above the water—sometimes in pairs in perfect synchronisation. These were magic minutes, the dolphins having so much fun. Pauline tried to catch them on the camcorder, but they move so quickly she was always on the wrong side, or just too late.

That afternoon the fresh wind continued, and we sailed along at a good speed. The chimneys of Sines were apparent long before we could see the town; two then three tall chimneys on the horizon. At first they

Lisbon to Lagos—in stages

appeared to be in the sea, but from the chart we could see that we had to go well to their west, although it is difficult not to aim for landmarks such as these.

In due course, the industrial area became visible, the smoke from the chimneys horizontal in the wind. It is on a fairly flat piece of land, but the town of Sines is on a bluff and became visible a little later. By now we could see a few ships; two were at anchor off the coast, while one was coming in to Sines, and another had left recently.

Sines is principally an oil terminal, but also has a commercial port and a marina which was built a couple of years ago, all behind large quays. However, the north quay terminates several hundred metres before the buoy one must round to enter the port. We knew from our winter reconnaissance that it was little more than a boat park. The harbour itself is very large with a wide entrance, the commercial port off to the south and the oil terminal on the north breakwater. The marina is right in the far corner.

By the time we were approaching Sines the swell was larger still and was now coming from the north-west. We took the sails down outside the port as we did not know just how much room there was inside. It was a bad decision because we were now head on into big waves, so the boat was leaping up and down as we lowered the sails. Before entering the harbour we had to wait a minute to avoid colliding with a large cargo vessel that was also coming in. Then we motored in and could see that the harbour was huge; there would have been plenty of room to come inside into the peace and calm before lowering the sails!

The marina is behind a pair of breakwaters that enclose a bay with a sandy beach opposite the entrance, a fishing harbour on the north side— but quite a distance up from the entrance—and the marina on the south side. As we passed between the two jetties, we could see a couple of yachts at anchor, and perhaps we should have joined them. Turning toward the marina we saw we had a choice; either to go straight into a pontoon or go around the end and turn back into the wind. Unfortunately, the channel at the end of the pontoons was rather narrow, and a large French-registered vessel, presumably a converted fishing boat was taking up a lot of the channel. It is normally best to come into the pontoon facing a strong wind—and the wind was still howling in behind us, but the problem was that we might not be able to turn in the space at the end without *Zefka's* bow being blown off by the wind. I could visualise us getting stuck in there somehow, and did not relish the idea.

Therefore I decided to go straight in. When still some distance away I put the lever into reverse. *Zefka* did not slow down! We were going too fast, but all I could do was push the throttle down to the stop. She started to slow up and, fortunately, a couple of Frenchmen from a boat nearby saw us and came running over to take the bow as we came in. Thanks to them we only scratched the paint a bit as we hit the pontoon; it could have been a lot worse!

The harbourmaster was on a pontoon nearby and came over to see how we were managing. I mentioned that the wind was a bit strong for coming in to the pontoon, and he smiled, replying, perhaps with a little too much satisfaction in his voice:

'It is like this *every* afternoon in August.'

He was very welcoming and friendly, and a good ambassador for the marina, which is actually not bad at all. Unfortunately, because of the proximity of the chemical complex, there is a lot of dust in the air, and the next morning the deck was covered with dirt once more. We did not go into the town, partly because it is some distance from the marina, and partly because when we had visited it in January we thought it reasonable but ordinary. It is best known as being the birthplace of Vasca da Gama the famous explorer.

19th July: A long day, but a marvellous one: dolphins, good wind, good sailing and glorious scenery

With about 75 miles to go, we were up by five o' clock, and moved astern off the mooring just after six. This is one of the stretches of coastline where there is no port of refuge at all until you turn around the cape at Portugal's south-western tip, and then you can shelter below the cliffs at Point Sagres. But we were heading for Lagos.

It was a still morning, but a little misty, and only just light. We are not at our best in the morning even at a reasonable hour, so we were both really grumpy as we raised the sails, but the mood soon passed. We motored out of the large harbour, and passed a couple of large ships anchored nearby. On the coast was another processing plant of some sort with a tall chimney belching forth smoke.

Owing to the mist, I decided to keep close to the coast rather than make for the first headland which sticks out a little, some 20 miles away. It was a good plan because, once we left the industrial area, the coastline improved, and we were to see some of the most beautiful scenery of the whole voyage, and certainly the most interesting coastline and sealife packed into one day. It all started quietly enough with some sand dunes, but after a while there were low sandstone cliffs with green foliage behind. We met a few fishing boats, and noticed a few very small harbours on the coast, each in a little indentation in the cliffs where a river met the sea. Alongside one was a beach with nice yellow sand.

With no wind whatsoever—and for once almost no swell—we took the foresail down after a while, and motored on, avoiding the numerous fishermen's floats and enjoying the scenery. At ten o' clock we passed Cape Sandao, but it was not until two o' clock that the sky cleared and the wind started to come—not quite like clockwork, but this had been the time for the wind to appear on so many days, it was becoming a habit. An hour later we were sailing along at five to six knots in front of a force three to four north-westerly wind over a slight swell on a fine sunny day. Several small groups of dolphins came to take a look at *Zefka*, but were clearly about some important business, because none stayed for more than a few seconds.

As we travelled further south so the cliffs became gradually higher, but there were also a few small sandy coves along the coast, and one or two looked very busy. Then we came to a couple of large beaches, each about a mile long, but evidently with access only by unmade roads. Following the next headland were a group of rocks about 50 metres long, quite clear of the shore—apparently uncharted—well away from the direct route south, but nevertheless a potential hazard.

Now, we were approaching Cape Sao Vicente, and our spirits were lifted by the beautiful scenery and the steady wind. The cliffs for the last few miles are remarkable for the lines of the strata of rocks. Some are at about 45 degrees, then they curve down to almost vertical, and then curve back up, marked by rows of deep clefts.

The Leisurely Route to the Med

For many miles now we had hardly seen any sign of habitation. Then suddenly, perched high on the top of the cliff about a mile from the cape, was a house. A single storey building, white with an orange roof. The sort of house you expect to see in a housing estate. But there it was, out on its own, swept by the gales every winter but bathed by the sun and sea breezes that day. Pauline was already busy filming the beautiful scenery. As she zoomed in on the little house she asked her parents: 'How would you like to live *there?*'

By now the swell was increasing, but we were going almost with it, so the motion was fine. At half past four, having covered 53 miles, we were off Cape Sao Vicente, and saw to our surprise that, as at Peniche, there was a tall rock standing in the sea just off the cape. Rounding this cape was an exciting moment. We had been heading south for a long time now and Portugal had seemed endless at times, particularly north of Lisbon. Now, we had actually arrived at the south-west tip of Portugal. After this we would be heading east along the Algarve and there was still enough time to get to the Med. Fantastic!

On the top of the cape is a big lighthouse, with a shiny orange roof. It is part of a large building, much like the Spanish ones. As we changed course around the cape, with the wind now behind, *Zefka* started to goose wing, and we gazed at the dramatic sandstone cliffs that extend to Point Sagres, a foretaste of what is to come later. Not far past the cape is a cave that has been burrowed out by the relentless action of the sea.

Just as predicted by Mr. *Magic Dragon*, the swell was diminishing. It was here that we experienced one of the highlights of our voyage. As we passed magnificent scenery, on a lovely warm sunny day, with the wind just perfect, a whole crowd of dolphins arrived. They stayed and played for about ten minutes, their mood obviously jubilant, matching ours. As before, two or more would dive and then leap together, crossing beneath the hull, and then swimming ahead as if they were an escort. Some would hang behind the boat, leaping out, and diving down, and swimming with amazing speed to go across beneath, behind or in front of the boat. This time Pauline pointed the camcorder at the sea beside the boat and waited for the dolphins to swim into view. There were so many and they stayed for so long that she was rewarded with some good shots of these lovely

Lisbon to Lagos—in stages

creatures. Not long after they had left I saw a flying fish suddenly emerge from the sea and fly in a low arc for about 50 metres before disappearing into the sea again. Pauline saw a whole shoal of tiny silver fish leap right out of the water; she surmised that they must have done that to avoid being caught by a dolphin or other predator. Now we were so glad that the strong winds had stopped us from sailing this beautiful part of the journey in the dark.

Just after Point Sagres, we glanced at the sheltered anchorage there and the small fishing harbour in the next bay. It was then that we realised the wind was strengthening; the usual late afternoon wind was coming. We reefed two panels; half an hour later, we reefed a third, and after another half an hour we were reefed down to just three panels and still sailed at over six knots.

The swell was definitely missing, but instead there were the steep, short waves, driven by the wind coming over the land, of the sort that are familiar to British sailors. Because the wind was now almost on the beam, periodically a little spray would be blown back off the bow wave into the cockpit. It was still sunny, although the wind made it seem a lot colder than an hour earlier. The wind continued to blow at around a force five or six for another hour or so, and we pressed on at a good speed, and rounded Point Piedade, the headland before Lagos, at about 8pm.

Well before we passed the point we could see tall buildings, which could have been Lagos. I realised that they were too far east, and on studying the chart saw that they were at Portimao. The entrance to the marina at Lagos is tucked into the west side of the bay, right beneath the sun at that time of day, which made it difficult to distinguish. To follow the course recommended by the marina we headed well out into the bay and then turned back; I doubt that this is strictly necessary but, with the sun making visibility difficult, I did not want to take any chances. Therefore, we saw, but were not close to, the amazing pillars of sandstone islands and rocks that are all along that side of the bay.

Eventually, after what seemed a very long time, we had lowered the sails, and motored between the two lights that mark the entrance to Lagos harbour. We followed the long and fairly narrow canal up to the marina

The Leisurely Route to the Med

Derek had sailed all around the Med with his partner, but in Turkey she decided she had had enough and left. Derek then sailed single-handed all along the Mediterranean, and eventually ended up at Lagos.

'I haven't been anywhere for two years,' he said with a grin. 'I know so many people here now that I am reluctant to move on. But I must just go out one of these days to make sure I can still sail.'

He said that one disadvantage with Lagos was the absence of anywhere to take the boat out of the water, and that he had taken his boat along to one of the Spanish ports to anti-foul it.

Later, I spotted a boat called *Faraway* in the marina. A mid-blue yacht with a strange rectangular-section wooden mast, it had been berthed not far from *Zefka* in Plymouth the previous year. I saw the owner, Pete, briefly, and it appeared that he had set up a business there as a marine electronics engineer and offered sundry other services. That evening we went to Mediterraneo, which is run by a British woman, and it was full, as are all the decent restaurants in Lagos at the end of July. We had some interesting food there, although it is not in the same class as Restaurante Italia.

On the way back we went to make some phone calls from the booth when we heard an American or possibly Canadian woman describing the Atlantic crossing they had just made, to someone back home.

'It's like giving birth. You soon forget how awful it was, but I'll never do it again!'

While waiting to use the phone we looked to see what was written on the phone card we had just bought. There was a heart on each side and above was written *'Dicionario amoroso'*—dictionary of love, I presume.

On one side were various expressions in nine different languages. The English was:

'Shall we go all the way?'

The Spanish was just:

'Hello cutey/sexy,' or something similar.

And in French:

'The day of glory has arrived: kiss me!'

On the other side were the replies:

'Only if it's in separate directions,' in English,

And the Spanish:

' Yes, yes, but keep your hands off me I'm a catholic.'

'You're nuts aren't you?' (I think) in French.

Nothing very shocking but this was in Portugal where not so long ago young girls were not allowed out alone. We did not manage to translate the Portuguese, perhaps it was very proper. If so, you can see what they think of the English!

During our last day in Lagos, we spent much time deciding where to leave the boat. I really wanted it to be left out of the water and phoned a few marinas between the Spanish border and Gibraltar without success. We already knew that, once in the Med, there is nowhere to leave a boat out of the water at a reasonable price for two hundred miles. So, in the end, I decided that if the boat had to stay in the water, it should be in the Med. After all we had set out to reach the Med on this voyage, so that is what we would do!

Chapter Fourteen

The last leg: Lagos to Estepona

23rd July: An uneventful passage along the south coast of Portugal, then overnight to Cadiz

IT WOULD have been fun to hop along the coast from Lagos to Cadiz. There are several marinas on the way and the rivers in the salt flats off Faro, where it is possible to anchor, looked interesting. Once at the Spanish border you have a choice of at least six marinas before Cadiz. Some people divert up the river Guadalquivir to Seville and even spend the winter there. But we settled for going straight from Lagos to Cadiz, cutting across the Gulf of Cadiz.

We were all set to leave at about 9am, but we reckoned without the red tape of the marina office and the fact that their computer decided not to print at that point. While I was waiting for this technicality to be sorted, I saw Derek who had come to study the weather forecast.

The Leisurely Route to the Med

'I do it every day,' he said. 'But Portuguese weather forecasts are abysmal.' I had to agree.

It was about half past ten before we left. Once again there was hardly any wind, and the visibility was poor. Visibility improved during the day, the sun soon burst through the clouds, and it became hot. The good news was that there really and truly was no swell, the sea was actually calm. The bad news was that we had to motor almost all day, with just a slight breeze from the south-west.

We passed the lovely little resort of Carvoeiro and the massive resort of Albufeira. All along the coast there was beautiful sandstone rock, in many places eaten away by the sea to produce strange shapes, and the golden sands which draw the crowds to the Algarve. In the afternoon the wind, such as it was, swung round to the west, and just after four o' clock we passed Vale de Lobo and Vilamoura. There, the land is flat before the salt flats that continue for many miles. Within them is a navigable river, with two branches, one going to Faro and the other to Olhau.

Around six o' clock we were off the mouth of the river and, as we passed, we were surprised to see that the entrance was very wide, the entrance lights were on large towers, and the lighthouse just behind was really tall; it was of French proportions. We looked in wistfully, thinking what fun it would be to explore the rivers.

A couple of hours later we were able to turn the engine off, but it was short-lived—the strong evening wind just did not appear—and we were then obliged to motor-sail until two in the morning. We had a good dinner, and then settled into our routine of two hours on and two hours off. Now that we were so far south the nights were much longer. It was dark by ten, and did not get really light until seven BST and Portuguese time) or eight o' clock Spanish time.

During the night we saw just a few ships, and most were further inshore except for a couple of fishing boats. It was a beautiful night; fine and clear, the moon lit up the sea and a multitude of stars looked down on us. The sea was pretty flat and a gentle breeze blew from the west. In the early morning, clouds started to gather, obscuring the moon and stars, so it became very dark, a little colder, and remained that way until dawn.

The last leg: Lagos to Estepona

By five o' clock we could see the lighthouse at Chipiona, and by half past seven other lights were visible, which all confirmed that we were actually on course for Cadiz.

Several ships were anchored out in the Bay of Cadiz as we made our way to Puerto America marina. From the information we had read, we had gained the impression that there would be very little room in the marina. But as we entered the docks and turned into the marina, we were surprised to find it was almost empty. We moored at quarter to ten after an uneventful passage of 110 miles, then collapsed into bed for a couple of hours sleep.

Cadiz is well worth a visit, but the marina was disappointing. The normal showers and toilets were out of order—or not quite completed, it was hard to tell which—and the temporary showers were ridiculous. Water would hardly come out of the shower head! Definitely the worst on the whole voyage.

We had more fun in town. From the marina it takes about ten minutes on foot to reach part of the elegant old town, where there is a nice little park and some massive old trees. Just past the ferry port, where car ferries leave for the Canaries, is the really old part, a maze of narrow streets in which there are little shops and some restaurants full of character. In front of the 'new' baroque-style cathedral is a fine square and there are several other smaller and friendlier squares in this part of the town. Cadiz has long been inhabited, and on the seaward side of the old town are some remains of a Roman theatre, and several other buildings and monuments of interest.

Cadiz was originally built on a small peninsula connected to the mainland by a narrow causeway. Inside the causeway is the huge bay that has provided a natural shipping harbour for centuries. The marina, port and old town are all on this small peninsula so you do not need to go far to see the sights. Along the causeway is a row of tall blocks of flats facing the sea and overlooking a long beach. Further across are the commercial parts of the city. We spent a pleasant afternoon in the town, and then were ready to move on the next day.

25th July: Down the coast from Cadiz, past Cape Trafalgar and into Barbate

Although we were now close to our destination, we knew that there could be some heavy sailing ahead. Because the Strait of Gibraltar acts as a funnel, the wind there is always a good deal stronger than elsewhere on

The Leisurely Route to the Med

the coast. So it is obviously a good idea to go with a favourable wind. But there is more to consider: there are some unusual and very strong current flows through the Strait created as the sea evaporates pulling water into the Mediterranean, but of course the flow is slowed down or reversed by the outgoing tide. Also, the current can flow in different directions in different parts of the Strait at the same time. For example, the flow might be outwards in the middle, and inwards near the coast.

All this means that timing is crucial; it is important to let the flow take the boat into the Strait, and arrive at Tarifa with plenty of time to reach Gibraltar with the favourable current. Although it is possible to sail directly from Cadiz to Gibraltar, the timing is so critical that it is not advised, and we would have needed to leave in the middle of the night to do so. Therefore, we opted to go first to Barbate, and time our departure from there to suit the Strait. This would give us two passages of around 30 miles.

It was a familiar story when we left Cadiz the next day; first we had to beat out against quite a swell and a reasonable wind, which dropped off when we turned south, so that we had to motor-sail most of the way. It was another hot day. Once we had left the city of Cadiz, we passed along a coast of salt marshes and beaches, with low hills behind.

By the time we approached Cape Trafalgar, we had switched the engine off, and were sailing. The cape is unusual in that there is a high cliff of sandstone, covered mostly in small pine trees, and then a short causeway out to a rock where the lighthouse is built. There is deep water alongside the cliff, but the shallows extend a little way out from the lighthouse. Squinting through the sunlight it was difficult to imagine how it had been in the famous battle fought here nearly two hundred years ago. But the rocks had been there, they would remember.

Once we had passed the cape, we could see into the bay around Barbate, and across to the beaches and low undulating hills beyond. It is actually a very pretty little bay, but spoiled by the long and ugly tuna fishing nets hung in the water. There are four cardinal buoys at the extremities of these nets, which extend from very near the harbour entrance for about a mile. The three outer cardinal buoys are mounted on old fishing vessels, painted matt black, and looking very much like the ships of death they are, not just to tuna fish but also to dolphins which can get caught in the nets and suffocate.

Naturally, we gave them a wide berth, heading between the nets and the harbour entrance. We could not see the inner marker until we were almost on it—it is a very small buoy. As we motored into the bay we saw a large yacht coming along the other side of the bay, beyond the nets. According to the pilot book you are supposed to go out around them when approaching from the east, so we watched with interest; for a moment they hesitated, then continued onward and we could see later that there is access both sides.

This yacht led us into the harbour along the nice wide channel. The two men in the cockpit looked cool in the shade of their large bimini, reminding us that we must make one for *Zefka*, and soon! The harbourmaster assumed that since we both flew the red Ensign we must be friends, and directed us alongside them. The boat was a Bavaria of about 45 feet in length, and we later discovered that the young man was the paid skipper of the yacht, the older man was the owner. As soon as they arrived in the harbour, the young man put out a doormat to ensure that no one came on board with dirty feet. In fact, when disembarking he always carried his shoes ashore so that he did not get any dirt on the decks. It was a beautiful boat and immaculate, making us feel just a little scruffy.

Actually, they were both very pleasant and helpful, the skipper resembling a younger version of Bill Gates. We did not go ashore that evening as we have been to Barbate several times, and knew that we could not expect to find much to eat there. However, the skipper of the boat next door told us that they had sailed over from Sotogrande, where the boat was moored, to dine at a well-known fish restaurant in the town. Whereupon the owner's wife and two daughters arrived having travelled over by road—presumably not keen sailors.

When I visited the office I found an excellent chart on the notice board showing the current through the Strait at various states of the tide. In a small boat you are supposed to keep near the Spanish coast and out of the shipping lanes which occupy the middle. That actually makes life easier, because the current changes direction more frequently in the middle than at the edge. By studying the chart, I was able to decide what time we should leave. Of course, there was also the wind to consider. A strong easterly wind, or levante, through the Strait would be difficult to cope with—we needed a wind from the west, a poniente.

The Leisurely Route to the Med

26th July: Shopping, followed by a bit of a clanger leaving Barbate, and afterwards plain sailing to Gibraltar—the gateway to the Mediterranean

First thing after breakfast, we set out to walk into the supermarket, which is just past the large and ugly fishing port; ugly it may be, but it is a major advance on the awful buildings in the old fishing harbour which was alongside a creek at the other end of town.

We had just passed the port when we came to a large area of waste land, where it appeared a fiesta had been held. There was rubbish of all sorts all over the area, and a dead dog by the road side; unfortunately not such an uncommon sight in the south of Spain.

At that moment a Mitsubishi Shogun drew up alongside us, and there was the owner of the boat next door offering us a lift! The car was already quite full with his wife, daughters and the skipper. Two were quickly dispatched to the rudimentary seats in the back so that there was room for us. They were all heading into town and kindly dropped us off at the supermarket, where we bought some essentials before walking back to the boat. We looked in the chandler's near the fishing port because it looked a good one; up to that point we had hardly seen a chandler on the whole voyage, and those we had seen concentrated more on fashionable clothes than anything else. This one looked useful, as it would need to be to cater for fishermen.

We timed our departure from Barbate so we would arrive at Point Paloma, which is where the Strait of Gibraltar becomes funnel shaped, around high water—2.30pm—when the current is flowing east at it strongest near the Spanish coast. It was a glorious sunny day, and the weather forecast from Tarifa suggested that we should expect force three to four generally, but five to six in the Strait, and from the west!

When we came to raise the foresail it did not quite go according to plan. I pulled on the halyard, and it just whirled around the winch without any resistance.

'The halyard's broken!' Pauline shouted.

I looked forward, and could see what had happened.

'No,' I said. ' The shackle's come undone!'

The last leg: Lagos to Estepona

We have quick release shackles on the halyards, and you have to release the shackle to remove the sail cover, and then replace it. I had removed the foresail cover that morning, so it was no use blaming anyone else! I went forward to see whether I could pull it down with the boat hook, but could not reach it from the deck. I also found that if I pulled on the rope instead of the shackle, which I did before thinking, the shackle went higher! Now that we were out of the harbour, there was a surprising amount of swell, so we had to go back towards the beach and anchor before retrieving the shackle. This involved balancing with one foot on the pulpit and stretching up with a boat hook while the shackle did its best to evade capture by winding itself ever more around the halyard, aided by the swell. I resolved to fasten the shackles more carefully in future!

With that little incident behind us, we set off about three-quarters of an hour later than planned. We looked back at the town of Barbate, which now has a nice promenade all along from the old fishing harbour to the west end of the town, and a long beach. It is usually criticised as being a dump in most tourist guides, but I rather like it. It has a nice old quarter, and is otherwise a pleasant if ordinary town, obviously marred by the old fishing port. At the east end, the creek ends in salt flats.

There were two places along this coast which we were now keen to find from the sea. The first was a little town called Zahara where we had stayed one night two winters ago. As we sailed along it was quite easy to identify by the shape of the land. Zahara is a really pleasant place with several hotels and a number of bars and small shops. Nothing special, but it has a nice atmosphere, and the beach that stretches for miles in either direction is beautiful. The camcorder managed to focus on the hotel where we had stayed, a little shaky but recognisable.

In winter the rolling hills behind Zahara look as if they could be in England, but at the end of July all the hills along this coast were either covered in scrub or burnt brown. Toward the end of the bay is the carcass of an ugly hotel which is a blot on the landscape, and must have been almost as bad when it was operating. A little further on, the hills rise up from the plain to form low cliffs, and among these cliffs are a number of large, well-spaced villas looking out to sea. Most had the traditional small Spanish gardens, which are more like yards filled with shrubs that can stand the heat.

The Leisurely Route to the Med

To my surprise, one house had a long and fairly flat garden—with a large, neatly mown lawn.

'Look!' I said to Pauline. 'That must belong to a Brit; no one else could be that fanatical about a lawn here in this heat!'

'There's another one a bit further on,' she replied.

The second place we were looking for was now in view; a village called Bolona where my daughter had been on a field study course from university. The location was chosen because of the exceptional flora there, wonderful in the spring by all accounts.

The land rises steeply here behind the coast and as we passed a rocky headland, Tarifa came into view, with rows of wind generators well placed to catch those strong winds we had been warned about. Not for nothing is Tarifa the most favoured spot for windsurfers. Pauline was more than a little apprehensive, even though we were now getting reliable weather forecasts from the station at Tarifa and they had announced that any wind would be behind us. We had heard so many tales of people not making it through the Strait. One man told us of crewing for a skipper who tried to get through the Strait with the wind against them and ended up in Morocco! Another man, who had been through twice, said that the first time he did nothing and, as they arrived off Tarifa, the boat was almost knocked over. So the second time he took two reefs in just before Tarifa to the amusement of his crew, until it became obviously necessary a few minutes later. So we were ready.

Today it was eerily different. It was hot and sunny, with just a light breeze, and by the time we had passed Point Paloma—about 45 minutes behind schedule—we were motor-sailing at five knots, but the current was pushing us along at another four knots to give us nine knots over the ground. With that speed we would soon knock a little off our deficit. The situation was the same at Tarifa, except there the sea was very confused as it was being squeezed into the Strait.

Pauline was expecting a hidden wind to appear at any minute and knock us flat, I think, just as the ancients reckoned that once you got past Tarifa you were leaving the world, and that there was no way back. That could be so in the winter with the prevailing easterly levante.

The last leg: Lagos to Estepona

I kept looking over my shoulder for wind, and sure enough a little wind did come up as we left the town behind and entered the Strait. We were able to turn the engine off and sailed at about four knots, fairly close to the shore so as to keep in the favourable current which was now giving us an extra two knots. And this was how we sailed through the Strait, although as usual the wind did strengthen as we proceeded.

About a mile after Tarifa there is a little lookout station on the top of the hill and it is here, we think, that is home to Tarifa Radio, which controls movement through the Strait and issues weather forecasts. As we passed, so they gave us the latest: 'Force two to three generally, with three to four in the Strait this afternoon,' came the voice over the VHF radio. This was the first time that the afternoon weather forecast had differed from that issued in the morning in the whole of Iberia, even though sometimes the weather in the afternoon was widely different from that forecast in the morning. We raised our hats to the guys of Tarifa Radio as we passed.

Close to the Spanish shore we were well clear of the shipping lanes, which were busy not just with cargo vessels but also with a surprising number of ferries operating between Algeciras and Tangier. In the distance we could see the intriguing mountains of Africa. On the Spanish side barren hills rise up from the shore, very grand and rugged.

We were now approaching Carnera Point at about six knots, and at last there it was—the Rock of Gibraltar—the Med! What an exciting moment that was!

When we turned into the bay, we were goose winging, and true to type, the wind increased, pushing us along at six and a half then seven knots. There was little swell as we overtook a yacht that had been ahead of us through the Strait, but there was a lot of heavy traffic. One ferry going in one direction, another in the opposite direction, and a couple of other ships heading for the ports as well. In addition, there were about half a dozen ships anchored off the town of Gibraltar.

With all this traffic, we were really surprised to see dolphins leaping through the water as they headed out to sea across our bow. Then, as we watched we saw baby dolphins trying to emulate their parents. These little chaps looked as if they were only about 600-800mm long, just miniature versions of the adults. They would start to leap out of the water, but not quite make it, or just make a short leap; really cute. Some were more skilled and managed quite respectable leaps. We later discovered that dolphins have been living in and around the Bay of Gibraltar for a long time, but their future is threatened by the ships and the pollution in the bay. Efforts are being made to track them and ensure that they are able to survive. It would certainly be a poorer place without them.

The relatively new Queensway Quay Marina had been recommended to us by one of our friends, and so we went there. It is right by the town and the facilities are good. The young skipper from the Bavaria yacht in Barbate agreed it was the one to choose but cautioned us about B pontoon where the swell can be bad as it is near the entrance.

'Go to D pontoon,' he advised.

The marina has been built in front of some new blocks of flats on what was formerly military land—the military harbour is still there, just a little further south behind the same breakwater. We called on the VHF and were offered a berth at the end of D pontoon. It seemed strange to arrive at an English speaking place after all that foreign travel. As we were coming to expect, someone was waiting on the pontoon to help us moor; there were no finger pontoons, just mooring lines again. We moored and looked around. The rock towered above us. This was where we had had in our sights for two months—here we were at last! We gave each other a big hug, and grinned like a pair of Cheshire cats. We had made it, and so far had really enjoyed our voyage, and all the places we had visited. *Zefka* had logged 1,706 nautical miles according to the GPS, and apart from a couple of thin cords breaking, she had just kept going reliably, safely, and with tremendous elan.

Although we soon discovered that Queensway Quay was an excellent marina, the cost to leave *Zefka* there would have been prohibitive. But too many boats get that far and then are left to rot in Gibraltar; we wanted to keep on sailing and get right into the Med. Wherever our boat was left, we would return to stay on her in the winter—it had to be somewhere we liked and truly Spanish.

The last leg: Lagos to Estepona

Still, the marina was a good place to spend a couple of days, and even the well designed blocks of flats behind were a pleasant backdrop. We think Gibraltar is a bit dreary, but some people like it. There is one main street through the town which is mostly full of shops selling duty-free electronic goods and souvenirs, generally hardly cheaper than in Spain. Most of the buildings are dull; almost like a Lancashire cotton town. There are some exceptions, of course, and these are mostly the official buildings. Often in the winter, cloud hangs over the rock when all around is clear and sunny.

One of the nicest places in the town is House of Saccarello, a restaurant where they serve light meals and have their own wide selection of excellent coffees. It has a lovely atmosphere. There is a small, rather poor Tesco supermarket in Main Street, but an excellent Safeway in the newly developed area outside the old fortified wall.

We spent a pleasant couple of days there, moored next to *Orion*, a 35-footer which had come from the Helford River a year before us. They had wintered the boat in the river Guadiana, which separates Portugal from Spain, and had been meandering down the coast for a couple of months. Their plans were rather different from ours. They wanted to sail around the Med during the summer and return to England each winter. Our idea was to spend the worst winter months in the Med and also a couple of months in summer, before it gets extremely hot and crowded, returning to the UK in between. However, many people we met had come to cruise around the Mediterranean for several years before returning home and some liked it so much that they are living there permanently on their yachts.

Almost all the boats in the marina were over 40 feet, and there was one huge motor yacht, about 100 feet long, which appeared to be registered in an Arab country. Mr. *Orion* learned that it had never moved in the three years it had been there, and the owner was in jail somewhere, believed to be in the UK. Nevertheless, people came to maintain the boat while we were there.

Our first job in the morning was to change our empty Camping Gaz bottle for a full one. Pauline asked in the office where that could be done, and she was directed to a firm called Rumagas in a new trading estate at the far end of the harbour.

The Leisurely Route to the Med

'Is that the nearest,' she asked innocently.

'It's the ONLY one,' came the reply. Gibraltar is a bit like that.

As we set off a light rain began to fall so we took our waterproof jackets, but thought it would just amount to a few spots. Instead, the intensity of the rain increased all the way up to the trading estate. We found the gas, and were surprised to find all sorts of stores there including a large DIY shed in buildings that had obviously belonged to the navy not long before. By the time we returned to the boat, we could just about wring out our trousers, they were so wet. That afternoon we heard on the radio that rain in July was absolutely unheard of in Gibraltar. We soon fixed that didn't we?

We were getting more adept at jumping off the bow onto the pontoon now, but I still looked at every device that might simplify the task, especially when carrying shopping. So it was that we fell into conversation with Jenny and Colin, a South African couple, who had been cruising in the Mediterranean for some years in a 43-footer. He had made a short ladder that was fitted permanently ahead of the anchor, and which seemed to work well. They had not been too lucky with other supplies, though. They had needed a special nut for the folding propeller, and had waited a month for it in Aguadulce, which is a couple of hundred miles further east along the Spanish coast. Then, Colin had decided to install a radio system so that he could send and receive e-mail from the boat, and thought that he would get this done much quicker in Gibraltar than in Spain. Not so, it seemed. Some of the work had been done, but instead of the job taking a week, as promised, it had already taken a month and was not quite finished. Colin also told us of one of those horror stories about getting a mooring in August.

'We had been sailing off Ibiza, and had anchored in a bay. It blew up very hard, and the anchor started to drag so we decided to go to the marina,' he told us. 'The marina was packed, and there were quite a few boats on the waiting pontoon. Nevertheless, we did not want to risk anchoring so we rafted up there for the night. They charged us 8,000 pesetas, and there wasn't even any water or electricity on the pontoon. Dreadful.'

Berths in marinas in Spain in the summer cost about 2,500 pesetas for a boat of that size, and about 4,000 pesetas in the Balearics, so that was quite a rip-off.

The last leg: Lagos to Estepona

We did not do any of the traditional tourist trips, such as going up the rock to see the barbary apes and the view. Perhaps if we had, our opinions of Gibraltar might have changed. But by the time we performed our essential chores, and had relaxed a bit, lethargy set in.

28th July: Winds round the rock, then a sedate cruise to the crowded marina at Estepona

Before we left Gibraltar, we heard the weather forecast, and up to then, Mr. *Orion* had said he would stay another day or two in Gibraltar. I told him that they were forecasting a westerly wind that day, with easterlies starting the next day. He did not comment, but went below as we left to fill the tanks with duty-free diesel. When one of the men running the business there found that *Zefka* was from Plymouth, he let out a cheer as he was a Plymothian.

Out in the bay, a fresh breeze was coming from the south-west, accompanied by a short choppy sea. We beat out to the south of the rock, threading our way past many ships at anchor. As soon as we were exposed to the full strength of the wind, it was clear we had too much sail up, so we turned and put two reefs in each sail. As we turned we saw the boat behind turn as well; it was *Orion*. The strong wind was very local, just whistling around the rock, and within an hour we shook out the reefs. The wind gradually diminished to nothing by the middle of the afternoon, the sea was very calm and we now wished we had a bimini to shade us from the hot sun. By this time we had passed the marinas of Sotogrande and Duquesa. We were well on our way to Estepona, which we had chosen as our final port because, unlike the others, it is on the edge of a small town. We hoped they would have room for us to leave *Zefka* there, as they had said they would when we phoned the previous day.

We drifted along at two or three knots under sail, and only started to motor when the speed dropped to almost nothing; we were in no hurry. But as it happened, our arrival was not well timed; we were the fourth of a string of yachts to enter the marina in as many minutes. When we entered, we found that the reception pontoon was occupied by a couple of small motor boats, which had been left while their owners had lunch in one of the restaurants.

The Leisurely Route to the Med

So we had to drift around the marina until it was our turn to be moored. The *marinero* put us between two large boats; an old motor cruiser and an old yacht. It was a bit of a squeeze getting into the space, with *Zefka's* fenders rubbing on one of the boats, but she went in easily enough.

This really was the end of our summer voyage. It was now almost the end of July, and we discovered, when organising a mooring for *Zefka* for the next six months, that almost all the spaces were booked up for August. This is evidently the way the Spaniards go sailing in the summer; they book a berth for a month and stay there. However, we were able to move to what appeared to be a better mooring, but that is another story.

We had left Fowey on 6th June, and arrived at Estepona on 28th July, having covered 1,731 miles on the way. Now we really could cheer and relax. But we did not want to leave the boat and return to England—we were ready to just keep sailing…….. Needs must, as they say, so we flew back from Gibraltar on 2nd August.

Afterword

Not only had *Zefka* sailed well, but our planning had been pretty good on the whole. The provisions we brought lasted almost the whole voyage, so that the only things we had to buy regularly were fruit, vegetables, bread and water. It would certainly have been foolhardy to come without all the charts we had brought, and needless to say the one showing the ports on the north-west coast of Spain, including San Ciprian was invaluable. A few more large-scale charts would have been helpful, but as it was we spent a small fortune on charts. We were very pleased to have the Seafile which was a tremendous help getting into harbours, but it only goes as far as Gibraltar so you need pilot books after that.

The awnings we made were complete disasters because they took so long to put up and take down, and we went back with ideas for simpler, Mark 2 versions. In fact, owing to the thick insulation in the hull of *Zefka*, awnings did not seem indispensable, and most of the time we did not use them—even when it was 32-35 degrees in the shade. On the other hand, we decided that we do need a good bimini and a cockpit table.

We had really enjoyed our voyage, despite our inauspicious start, the bad weather we hit and the few mishaps. It is the most fabulous two months we have spent together—just fantastic. We are now much more of a team than before we left in all respects, not just sailing, and once we were into the rhythm of sailing, we just wanted to keep going. We can heartily recommend it!

But let Pauline have the last word:

To any women who are not experienced sailors, but are considering crewing from England to the Med or the Algarve: if you have read this book you will realise by now that I get scared in rough weather. In fact, I squeak quite loudly at times. However, I can honestly say that I would do it again. With this experience behind me, I have gained confidence in myself and the boat so I am now much happier when the wind blows up.

So, if, like me, you are less than brave, don't consider a three-day passage across the Bay of Biscay where you have nowhere to hide if the weather turns nasty—which it often does. Do the coastal route where you will hardly ever be far from a harbour, and you can more reliably time your crossings to coincide with reasonable weather. And finally do not be tempted to sail to a very tight schedule. We saw and heard how keeping to schedules resulted in people having frightening experiences. Give yourselves plenty of time, more than we had if possible, then sailing to the Med can be a wonderful experience. And it's only just the beginning! Happy sailing.

THE ROUTE:
Plymouth to Estepona

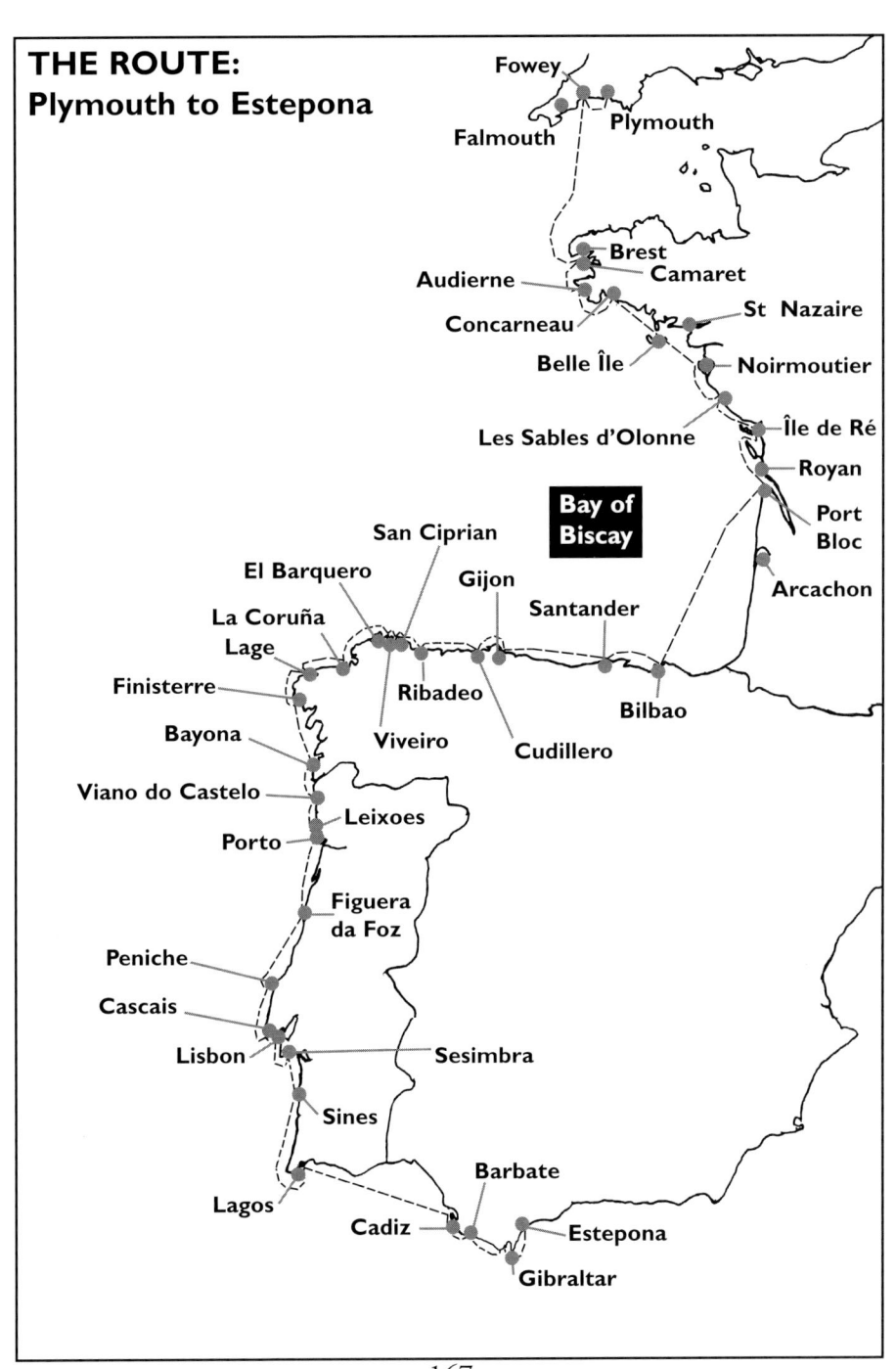

Part Two:
Preparation for the voyage

Chapter Fifteen

Ports of call: Plymouth-Estepona

FROM MOST of the English coast, we recommend that you head for Falmouth and cross the Channel from there to the north-west of France. The advantage of this approach is that your first passage or two will be along familiar coasts, and should you need to buy some parts or get some changes made, it will be easier than along the French coast. If you start in the Solent and head straight for France, your cross-Channel passage will be shorter, but you will then sail into the prevailing wind all the way along the French coast to Brittany, and deal with some very strong currents in some places.

Falmouth-Le Conquet is the shortest passage from the south-west, but the inner harbour at Le Conquet is suitable only for small boats that can dry out. Larger boats must anchor outside the harbour in less protected waters. Therefore, Camaret is the popular destination for most cross-Channel skippers coming from the West Country. Once across the

The Leisurely Route to the Med

Channel, there is a big variety of ports of call, and quite a number of suitable anchorages as well. The bay behind the breakwater at Audierne is easy to find and enter, and so is the marina at Concarneau. The alternatives of Benodet and Loctudy are a little more difficult, owing to the fast currents that can flow, and if you have time, Douarnenez is not far away. La Forêt is another big marina on this coast. Thereafter, you can follow the island route as we did, or stick to the coast, which will take longer. Of course, if you have plenty of time, you can visit the islands and the coast. The coastal route will take you to the Morbihan, one of the most renowned French cruising grounds with plenty of anchorages. Either way, you will enjoy some good cruising. There are about eight marinas to choose from between the Morbihan and Noirmoutier.

Further south, there is an alternative for just about every port we visited. Most crews would want to enter La Rochelle and visit the city. We did not do so, partly because the tides were unfavourable, and partly because we were keen to visit the Île de Ré. We did not have time for both, but had found on a previous visit that La Rochelle is an attractive and interesting city.

Further south, Rochefort, several miles up a river, is about the only marina before the mouth of the Gironde. Most skippers head for Royan where there is a large marina, but Port Bloc is a simple marina run by friendly people, and it saves a few miles. However, facilities are poor, and the shops in the village are rather far from the marina. Of course, you can take the ferry over to Royan, which has good facilities and shops, we understand.

Because Jon wanted to go back to the UK by train, we headed for Bilbao from Port Bloc, since it was nearer the French border and would save him time. Otherwise we would have headed directly to Santander, which has a fairly sheltered entrance, and which is just a few miles further than Bilbao. An advantage of the route to Santander is that you head further out from the French coast, so that should bad weather blow up you have more searoom. If the weather were to blow up near the Spanish coast, it would be possible to divert into Bilbao or another port in that area. Bilbao is the easiest to enter, although it would also be possible to shelter off Laredo.

Ports of call: Plymouth-Estepona

The voyage from Royan to Gijon is a good deal further, and the biggest problem of the Bay of Biscay is that the weather can change very quickly and long-range weather forecasts are unreliable. Therefore, Royan-Santander is the optimum corner to cut as you are much less likely to be hit by bad weather than going directly across the Bay of Biscay. We do not advise the direct route because almost everyone we met who had done so had had a very uncomfortable time. Indeed, one skipper had such a terrible time that when they arrived in Spain he flew back to England, leaving the boat to his paid crew to take down to the Med. His wife had wisely not joined them for that part of the voyage.

We understand that in July and August there is no firing out to sea, so you can make the passage of about 70 miles from Royan to Arcachon—the last ten miles are in the sheltered estuary. It is another 60 miles to Capbreton, and then a short hop of 30 miles to San Sebastian, compared with about 75 miles to Bilbao. Because you will be close to a lee shore on this route, do pay attention to the weather forecasts.

If you set out from the Gironde to Santander, when you get 20-30 miles from the Spanish coast, you could turn south-east and head into the little ports near the Spanish/French border. San Sebastian, Lequeito, Castro Urdiales and Laredo are all interesting, although most are small.

From Santander, there are a few small ports, but these are limited either in depth or when you can enter. Llanes, which is about half way, has an inner basin with a lock, while there may be space in Lastres. Gijon is an excellent port, which can be entered in any weather, and is also an interesting city. It has a large visitors' marina. Further on, Cudillero can be entered in most weather, and is well sheltered, although some swell can come in. Once in Galicia, the rias offer good shelter and interesting cruising—there are six rias between La Coruña and Bayona. These days, the northern Portuguese coast has marinas at reasonable intervals—Viana do Castelo, Povoa de Varzim—which suffers from the westerly swell, we're told—Leixoes, Figueira da Foz, Nazare, Peniche and Lisbon.

It is a long haul from Sines to Lagos, however. Anchorages are few and far between along the Portuguese coast, and also on the Atlantic coast of the south of Spain. However, there are plenty of marinas between Lagos and Gibraltar. These include Portimao—a new marina—Vilamoura and

173

Vila Real de San Antonio in Portugal, with anchorages near Faro and Olhau. Along the Spanish coast there are marinas at Ayamonte, Isla Christina, Huelva, Mazagon, Chipiona and four more in the Bay of Cadiz. Incidentally, eight of those between Ayamonte and Barbate are operated by Puertos de Andalucía. If you visit more than one, take you receipt from the previous of their marinas, and you will save a bit of time in the office.

To time your arrival at the Straits of Gibraltar, we recommend stopping at Barbate, where there is an excellent chart in the office with details of the currents through the Straits at all states of the tide. In Gibraltar there are three marinas, Queensway Quay, which is nearest to the town, Shepherds and Marina Bay which are next door to one another. Shepherds has an excellent chandlers. Of course, one of the attractions of Gibraltar is that equipment and fuel for the boat are duty-free.

PORTS OF CALL PLYMOUTH-ESTEPONA

Date	From	To	Distance sailed
6 June	Plymouth	Fowey	29.6 nm
7-8 June	Fowey	Camaret	135 nm
9 June	Camaret	Audierne	28.5 nm
10 June	Audierne	Concarneau	39.8 nm
11 June	Concarneau	Belle Île (buoy)	48.1 nm
12 June	Belle Île	Noirmoutier	41.7 nm
13 June	Noirmoutier	Les Sables d'Olonne	48.7 nm
14 June	Les Sables d'Olonne	St Martin, Île de Ré	26.0 nm
16 June	St Martin	Port Bloc	58.0 nm
17-19 June	Port Bloc	Bilbao	170 nm
20 June	Bilbao		
21 June	Bilbao	Santander (buoy)	38.8 nm
22 June	Santander		
23 June	Santander	Gijon	81.4 nm
24 June	Gijon		
25 June	Gijon	Cudillero	29.5 nm
26 June	Cudillero	Ribadeo	48.2 nm
27 June	Ribadeo	San Ciprian (anchor)	33.2 nm
28 June	San Ciprian	Viveiro (Celeiro)	12.0 nm
29 June	Viveiro	El Barquero (anchor)	15.2 nm
30 June	El Barquero	La Coruña	48.1 nm
31 June-2 July	La Coruña		
3 July	La Coruña	Lage (anchor)	38.5 nm
5 July	Lage	Finisterre (anchor)	42.4 nm
6 July	Finisterre	Bayona	55 nm
8 July	Bayona	Viano do Castelo	31.8 nm
9 July	Viano do Castelo	Leixoes	31.1 nm
10 July	Leixoes	Figueira da Foz	63.7 nm
11 July	Figuera da Foz	Peniche	59.3 nm
12 July	Peniche		
13 July	Peniche	Cascais (anchor)	48.5 nm
14 July	Cascais	Lisbon Alcantara	14.2 nm
15-16 July	Lisbon		
17 July	Lisbon	Sesimbra (anchor)	32.4 nm
18 July	Sesimbra	Sines	32.3 nm
19 July	Sines	Lagos	74.9 nm
20-22 July	Lagos		
23-24 July	Lagos	Cadiz	109.6 nm
25 July	Cadiz	Barbate	33.8 nm
26 July	Barbate	Gibraltar	29.7 nm
27 July	Gibraltar		
28 July	Gibraltar	Estepona	21.6 nm

Total distance by GPS 1731.5 nautical miles; by log 1651.2 nautical miles.

Comments	Alternative ports
(Good shelter unless stated otherwise)	
Easy entrance, nice town	Falmouth
Easy entrance	Le Conquet
Care needed, nice town	Audierne
Easy entrance, interesting old town	Benodet, Loctudy, La Foret
Beautiful island, lovely town	Port Haliguen
Don't enter or leave at low water!	Pornic, Saint Nazaire
Easy entrance, nice town	Ports La Vie & Bourgenay
Easy entrance, beautiful place	La Rochelle
Limited depth at low water in moorings; poor facilities	Royan
Easy entrance; superb but expensive marina	Santander, Arcachon, Capbreton
Interesting city - go in on the underground	San Sebastian, Guetaria
Wide entrance, some care needed	
Very interesting city	Castro Urdiales & Laredo
Pass the town before turning into the port	Several small harbours
Lovely city	
Refuge - no facilities	
Some care needed with entry in identifying marks	Luarca
Good well sheltered anchorage; dangers outside marked	
Straightforward	
Anchorages only; well sheltered	
Easy entrance	Ria de Cedeira
Fine city with Torre de Hercules lighthouse	
Very safe anchorage	
Excellent anchorages	Corme
Superb marina, nice old town	Corcubion
Watch tide just outside marina; nice town	Two rias, Vigo
Easy entrance, good marina	Povoa de Varzim
Very tricky cross-current just inside marina	
Easy entrance, good shelter, swell from fishing boats	Aveiro, Nazare
Interesting place	
Good anchorage in northerlies	
Easy entrance	Santo Amara, Terreiro do Trigo
Very attractive city, marina very near	
Good anchorage in northerlies	
Easy entrance; watch wind when approaching pontoons	Setubal
Easy entrance, but strong current near reception pontoon	
Superb marina, tourist town	Anchor at Sagres, marina at Portimao
Easy entrance; interesting city	
Easy entrance; town distant and uninteresting	Several
Easy entrance	
Interesting place, good facilities	
Easy entrance; very nice town	Marbella, Fuengirola

Chapter Sixteen

The sort of boat you need

FOR THE cruise to the Med, you need a seaworthy boat of reasonable size that rides comfortably through bad weather. Of course, you can make the passage in a boat of any almost any size, but even for one person a 23-footer is about the minimum. We met a German couple who had spent six years sailing around the world in a 30-footer, and people do sail to the Med in much smaller boats. However, if you intend to live aboard, 30 feet is probably the minimum comfortable size, and very few people seem to attempt this voyage in anything smaller. Most of the boats we met on the way, and in the Med, were 35-45 footers. The original owner told us that *Zefka* was what they and the designer considered to be the smallest boat suitable for long-distance cruising. Owing to its short overhang at the bow and counter stern, it is spacious for its size. After leaving Vancouver in 1986 they sailed *Zefka* across the Atlantic and around the Mediterranean for an extended voyage lasting seven years.

The Leisurely Route to the Med

In deciding on what length of boat to buy, it is worth taking into account the fact that marinas on the continent charge per metre. In almost all cases, the steps are 8, 10, 12, and 15 metres; in some cases, steps of 14 and 16 metres replace the one for 15 metres. The extra cost for a boat of 10.1 or 12.1 metres—33ft 1in or 39ft 8in—compared with 9.9 metres and 11.9 metres respectively adds up to quite a lot over a year.

Ideally, you want a boat no more than 32ft 8in or 39ft 4in or 45ft 10in. The price of a marina berth for a 12-metre yacht is usually 20-35% more than for a 10-metre boat, and the increase between 12 and 14 metres is similar. Also, a 35-footer with a long overhang at the bow and retrousée stern will not only cost a lot to moor, but may have no more storage space than a less sporty 30-footer. It is not necessarily best to buy the biggest boat you can afford; you may do better to buy a slightly smaller boat that is spacious for its size and which you can afford to equip as you want.

Most boats will do, but the heavier displacement yachts, intended primarily for cruising, fit the bill well—not just for the voyage to the Med, but also for sailing when you get there. Many people expect to meet only light winds in the eastern Mediterranean, but this is far from the case. Even in the summer, the wind can blow up very quickly, creating quite big seas, and these storms can last for some time. Gales are prevalent in the Golfe du Lion in the north of the Mediterranean for most of the winter, and occur quite frequently at other times, affecting the weather south of the Balearics. Therefore, lightweight semi-racing boats, epitomised by some modern French yachts, make life pretty uncomfortable even in a swell, according to people who had experienced them. Motor-sailers, which have wheelhouses without any cockpit to speak of are generally not recommended, unless they are very spacious. You do need plenty of fresh air in the hot Mediterranean summer.

A day's passage in the Med often starts with no wind or light airs, which gradually increase, so it is an advantage to have a large sail area that can be reefed easily. From our observations, boats that are awkward to reef spend a lot of time motoring—even when they have a following wind.

Good engine essential

A good engine is also essential. It is not that you need power to fight the currents, as around Brittany, but that you need a reliable engine which

The boat you will need

starts easily and runs effortlessly for long periods when there is no wind. A reasonable amount of power is clearly an advantage in bad weather. Ease of maintenance is also important, as you will probably want to carry out routine maintenance yourself. Service for Volvo engines is available in or near almost all ports, and Perkins engines have been used for many years in Ebro vans and small trucks (now Nissan) so parts for these are available cheaply in Spain.

For other engines it is best to take some spares, and to find the part numbers for the equivalent oil and fuel filters for cars or trucks, since these are cheaper and easier to obtain than those for marine engines. Since they are fairly light, you could get filters sent out, or take them out when you travel by air between the Med and the UK as you will almost certainly do from time to time.

The layout

Zefka has a rather unusual layout, with the heads in the forepeak, then a large sleeping cabin with big double berth and plenty of storage space, and a main cabin with two more berths and a good chart table. More to the point, the main cabin is spacious and has a good galley. We love the layout, at sea and in ports. A chart table is obviously necessary, but it does not need to be very large, although plenty of space for storing charts is necessary.

A sleeping cabin that is separate from the main cabin is a distinct advantage if you are to spend much time on a boat—essential in our view—and you need as much storage space as you can find for your money. Large fuel and water tanks are worth paying extra for, particularly if you plan to anchor regularly rather than use marinas—*Zefka* was well equipped in this respect.

Another overlooked but important feature is insulation. If you are fitting out a boat yourself, put in as much insulating foam as you can. If you are buying a used boat, look for one that is well-insulated. *Zefka* has a thick coat of foam which keeps the cabins relatively cool even without the use of awnings. If the boat has poor insulation, a light colour paint or gel coat for the topcoat and decks helps prevent the boat becoming too hot. A white deck reflects too much dazzling light, though, so beige or another light colour is preferable there.

Because the Mediterranean is more salty that the English Channel—and the amount of salt increases as you go east—large anodes are essential. Standard ones can be bought easily and cheaply in the Med, but if your boat has some special anodes, take a few spares. Anti-fouling also needs to be of good quality owing to the abundance of shellfish and seaweed.

Of course, good padlocks are essential these days not just for the hatch and lockers but also for anything of value left out on deck.

Anchors

Once you are in the Med you are likely to anchor a lot, so make sure that the anchor is easy to use and that there is room to stand at the bow while you or your crew is operating the windlass. It should also be easy to attach the chain to the Sampson post or main cleat so that the load is taken off the windlass.

Anchors are most important, and must be heavy enough to do the job in strong winds, which can blow up unexpectedly. *Zefka* is equipped with three anchors: A45lb CQR, a 50lb FOB Brittany anchor, and a 15lb Danforth-type as a kedge. The CQR is brilliant in most seabeds, and also breaks out well. The FOB Brittany anchor, which has a heart-shape plate but with two points is best in the combined sand and seaweed beds that are common in the Med. The seaweed is more like very coarse grass than weed, and many anchors including the CQR, can skid across it, but the FOB digs in well. A kedge is essential when mooring in Greek marinas, since there are no mooring lines. It also makes a useful stern anchor to hold the boat facing the swell in narrow bays—and can be used to pull a boat off a sandbank. Plenty of chain is needed to hold the anchor shank horizontal. About 50 metres of chain is just enough on the main anchor, allowing you to anchor fairly safely in a blow in a depth of 10-12 metres. If there is room for an extra 20 or 30 metres, so much the better.

In really windy conditions, some sailors put out two anchors about 30 degrees apart, but a simpler solution which evidently works very well is to attach the second anchor and about 10 metres of chain to an eye on the main anchor. With the two anchors in line, there is plenty of holding power, and the operation is simpler. Of course, this method will not prevent the boat sheering around.

Chapter Seventeen

Electronics and other equipment

DESPITE the trend toward the use of masses of electronics, which can consume quite a lot of power, you can make the voyage without anything more than the usual instruments. A GPS navigator was installed in *Zefka* when we bought her, so we used it, initially to check the position we had taken by hand bearings, but later as the main navigating tool. The GPS showed clearly when we moved out of the area used by the French for firing exercises in the Bay of Biscay, which was well worth knowing. Otherwise, we would have been guessing. We also appreciated it in the fog off the north of Spain.

Along the Portuguese coast there are few suitable navigation points for long stretches, and many of those you see are not marked on Admiralty charts—this is also the case along the south coast of Spain. Again, the GPS was very useful, but most of the ports are fairly easy to find. If the weather is fine and you are making a passage of 40-50 miles between substantial ports you don't really need to know precisely where you are. Nevertheless, GPS units are now relatively cheap, so at least a handheld one is worth having—had *Zefka* not been equipped with a GPS, we would have taken one.

Obviously, a VHF radio, depth sounder, log and speed indicator are virtually essential these days, and we would not be without our auto pilot. Many people use a wind-vane steering gear, but since our solar panel can power our auto pilot we did not take one. They occupy a lot of space when not in use, and of course can't be used when there is no wind—and we had quite a few days or half days without wind. Also, we did not envisage making any passages of more than two or three days at sea.

The Navtex weather information receiver was invaluable along the French coast, but after that we received very few broadcasts until we reached the Med. The Portuguese weather forecasts we received were of very little use —except in regard to the height of the swell. They repeat the morning forecast all day, even when it has been shown to be patently inaccurate!

The weather station at Tarifa issues good forecasts, and although the Spanish forecasts seem fairly reliable, they don't show up as often on the Navtex as they should. The French and the British issue the best forecasts, in our experience. Some experienced sailors rely on a multi-band radio, which can pick up the BBC forecasts as far as La Coruña and would be useful for picking up French forecasts in the Med. A conventional car radio with a good aerial can't. I definitely recommend one of these.

Because you are likely to use a lot of electric power, an ammeter to indicate the rate of charge of the alternator, and voltmeters to indicate the state of the batteries are pretty near essential. These instruments are not too reliable, so a multimeter, which can also help trace faults, is a recommended piece of kit.

Safety equipment

Of course, flares and life jackets are essential, but so are safety lines running along the decks. You never know in what conditions you might need to go onto the foredeck to fix some problem or other. EPIRBs are recommended; but if you rely on the small 121.5Mhz type it is best to carry two; apparently so many are let off accidentally, that unless two are heard in succession, some emergency services are said not to take much notice.

Electronics and other equipment

Cleats, fairleads and gantries
Particular attention should be paid to the cleats. Heavy-duty bow and stern cleats and fairleads are needed when mooring bow-to—or stern-to—because the ropes tend to be under quite high loads, pulling outwards at an angle from the boat. Breast cleats are not so important with these moorings, but when a strong wind is blowing the boat away from the pontoon, some skippers run a pair of warps from the breast cleats to the pontoon.

Many boats used for long-distance sailing have large gantries above the pulpit to carry all sorts of paraphernalia such as aerials, wind generators and solar panels. We keep our solar panel forward of the main hatch and move it around as necessary, but mounted on a gantry it would be always in the sunlight and out of the way of thieves—theft can be a problem in the Med as elsewhere. Many wind generators are noisy, and certainly need to be well out of the way of the crew, so if you plan to carry this sort of equipment, consider having a gantry made.

Pressurised water
Pressurised hot and cold water systems are common on larger boats these days, and we would certainly recommend one—the installation needs to be done with care and good components, though. With the hot weather, and the joy of swimming from the boat in clear water you need showers more than in the UK, so a pressurised system must be high on the wish list. It was one of the things we had installed in *Zefka* in our preparations for the voyage.

Pressurised water, with a gas heater and shower, gives you much more independence, and you don't need to go into marinas as much as you would otherwise do. Some people are nervous of gas water heaters, but the modern units are equipped with sensors and shut-off valves to shut down the supply if they overheat or the ratio of gas to air is incorrect. You do need gas sensors and alarms as a backup.

Auxiliary electric power
Shore power is recommended because electricity is included in the mooring fees in all French and most Spanish marinas. Because the sea is a good deal more salty in the Mediterranean than in the English Channel,

care is needed in the installation to avoid galvanic corrosion. Solar panels are now very efficient, and are useful, particularly if you intend anchoring a lot. They provide a reasonable amount of power silently, and of course, there is plenty of sun in the Med, even in the winter.

Conventional wind generators are noisy, and if not mounted well out of the way, can be dangerous. The type with a vertical axis are quieter, and can be mounted well out of the way up the mast on a boat with conventional rigging. They are very compact, and the concept looks the best, but we have no experience of either type. A battery charger, either built-in, or a portable type intended for cars, allows you to use the shore power in the marina to your heart's content. Essential if you have a fridge.

Gas cylinders
Although it is possible to have Calor gas bottles refilled in major cities and marinas, the places where this can be done are few and far between. Life is much easier if you equip the boat to take Camping Gaz cylinders, because these are available almost all over Europe and are very cheap in Spain. Unfortunately, cylinders are rarely available in the marinas—they don't seem to have that idea of service on the Continent—so you normally need to walk into town to an ironmonger—*ferreteria* in Spanish. The valves and piping can be obtained from caravan equipment shops in the UK. Of course, you need at least two cylinders.

Spanish gas is an even cheaper alternative than Camping Gaz, but because the smallest cylinder is at least 18 inches high, you need a large gas locker. A unique valve, which must be bought from the suppliers, Repsol, is used. To buy one, it used to be necessary to have an address in Spain, but that may no longer be the case. The smallest bottles are too large for most boats, unless you leave them out in the cockpit, which is one option for permanent live-aboards—in Spain only of course.

Refrigerators
In the hot atmosphere of the Mediterranean, a refrigerator enables you to keep your food fresh—important for your health. When we bought her, *Zefka* was equipped with a Supercool Peltier-effect refrigerator in the coolbox. These are not as efficient as fridges running on compressed refrigerant, but they use less current—6 Amps at full load on quick-cool,

and about 1.5 Amps on economy, which we use almost always. We tend to use the fridge when the engine is running and when hooked up to mains power in a marina with the batteries on charge.

Compressor-driven fridges which incorporate a holding plate are the most efficient. They are operated at full power when the engine is operated in the morning and evening, and evidently that is sufficient to keep food cold for 24 hours a day. They are expensive, and take up a lot of space. Compressors can be noisy, and of course any fridge discharges heat as it cools, so the outlet needs to be routed so that it does not heat up the cabin.

Awnings and biminis
An awning seems essential in the Med, and is not too easy to rig up with the junk rig owing to the absence of shrouds. We are now on our Mark II design, which consists of two pieces of thin coated nylon which run along each side of the booms. We can use some stainless steel tubes left over from the Mark I design to hold the outer edges of the material up so that the awning is near horizontal. A horizontal awning presents the minimum windage, but on the other hand, an awning shaped like a ridge tent provides a little more protection from the heat of the day. Ideally, it should be possible to mount the awning in either position.

Some awnings have curtains that hang down at the sides about 300mm, which improves protection against the evening sun, but still enables you to walk comfortably along the decks. Because you are more likely to moor bow-to, you will need easy access along one side of the decks fore and aft.

After our first season in the Med, we decided that a bimini was probably more important than an awning. The bimini not only makes a tremendous difference to the temperature in the cockpit on hot, airless days but also prevents the hot sun from beaming into the cabin—this sort of talk sounds a bit unrealistic when you are used to British weather, but the heat in the Med can be amazing, even at sea.

In fact, we did not finish our bimini before we left, so we just hung the material cut out for it over the boom to improve the situation in the cockpit when in the marina. An alternative is a large sunshade, preferably one with a tilt mechanism in the pole. These can be obtained cheaply in Spain.

One other useful piece of equipment is a cockpit table, because much of the time you can eat outside. We made a simple one with folding legs—found in a caravan and camping shop. It can be stowed beneath the cushions of one of the berths in the main cabin.

During the summer, it is hot enough to swim from the boat in most parts of the Med, so a bathing ladder is essential, and of course, boats with sugar-scoop sterns come into their own.

Passarelles and ladders

Many will tell you that a passarelle is an essential piece of equipment in the Med, but that depends on your level of agility. In most marinas, and with the layouts of most modern yachts, it is fairly easy to lower yourself off and clamber up at the bow. A passarelle is definitely an advantage, but is not essential. Of course, if the lady of the boat likes to go out to dinner in a skirt, a passarelle will come quite high on the list of essential equipment, as will a divided pulpit with space to walk through!

There are various alternatives to the passarelle. Some boats have a short ladder that hangs down two or three feet from the bow, and these work well so long as you can moor close to the pontoon. The cheapest way to make a passarelle is to buy a ladder about 1.5 metres long, place a pair of castor wheels on one end, and plywood along one face. Short ladders can be bought in some ferreterias in Spain.

Bicycles and rucksacks

We did not take bicycles with us, but decided that we did need some later on—they would have been useful in about half the ports we visited. In several cases, the marina is quite a distance from the town, and in others it is a long walk just to get off the marina. We also heard of people being held up by bad weather for four days or more at a time, and in that situation bicycles would make the stay much more enjoyable.

There are now plenty of folding bicycles to choose from, and most fold up into remarkably small packs. To go anywhere far off the marina, you will need three speeds, and preferably six. Ease of stowage is important, but so is ease of use when cycling; some of those with very small wheels are not too stable. We plan to buy some soon.

Electronics and other equipment

Rucksacks enable you to carry quite heavy shopping—not to mention gas bottles—easily. They are useful on foot, when going ashore by dinghy, or when cycling, leaving your hands free. It is surprising how much weight you can carry comfortably in a quite a small rucksack.

Mobile phones

If you want to contact a Spanish marina you will almost certainly get a response by phone, but are not likely to do so on the VHF. Therefore, a mobile phone is very useful, particularly since the Spanish lifeboat service has a phone number you can call in an emergency.

To cut the cost of the calls, it is best to use a pay-as-you-go service and a phone that can take any make of SIM—the electronic chip provided by the phone company. Some phones can operate with only the SIM provided when bought, but others can use any SIM. So long as you purchase one that can take any SIM, you will be able to buy one in Spain or Portugal, insert it in your phone and use the local service. They are very cheap there. If you are planning to spend a lot of time in the Med, it may be better to buy the phone in Spain, but make sure that it can take any SIM. You can now buy SIMs in the UK for pay-as-you-go phones in many specialist shops.

Solar shower

One of the most useful and inexpensive things we bought was a solar shower. It is simply a large black, plastic bag with a pipe and nozzle. Once filled with water it heats up in a few hours, although it takes a bit longer when you are on the move because the wind cools it. We didn't think of using it on the way down, but have found it provides two good showers in the Med in the summer. For about ten pounds, these are really worthwhile, and are available at most caravan equipment shops and some marinas in the UK.

Windscoop

The Windscoop is actually a registered name for a device that scoops the air into a hatch. There are some alternative designs, and they seem to get the air moving inside the boat. Once you have erected your awning, not much wind comes in through the hatches normally, so a Windscoop looks like a good idea. We did not take one with us, but intend to buy one before next season.

Torches and lights

A selection of torches are also useful. If your boat is not equipped with an anchor light, take a portable one that can be run up the mast—if you anchor regularly a good anchor light is good insurance. Some people think they don't need to use one in a quiet bay, but should a yacht collide with your boat in the dark and you are not showing an anchor light, you will be responsible. In fact, it is a good idea to have one as a spare as it is not always convenient to shin up the mast to replace a bulb.

Those end-on moorings

One of the daunting aspects of mooring in the Med, and in some marinas on the way, is the absence of finger pontoons. With these moorings, you tie up end on to the pontoon, and pick up a rope and tension it to hold the boat off the pontoon. The first we met was at La Coruña, and this system is also used at Bayona, Lisbon, Gibraltar and most Spanish marinas. One good feature of Spanish marinas is that they send a man round to help you moor, which is more useful with these moorings than with finger pontoons.

Most of the pilot books and many guides to cruising in the Med tell you to moor stern-to when there are no finger pontoons. Unless you have a very short fin keel and deep rudder—not a common specification for deep sea cruising—going astern is not easy, and is made much more difficult by winds and current. The best thing to do is to ignore this advice altogether, and to go in bow-to. I have seen so many experienced sailors get into an awful mess just because they decided to go into a berth stern-to when a cross wind was blowing—and when it wasn't for that matter. Moving out of these moorings astern is usually easy, so long as you go slowly.

The advantages of being bow-to are many. First, you have much more privacy, because people on the pontoon cannot see straight into the cockpit and main cabin. Secondly, most Mediterranean cruisers with

Electronics and other equipment

whom I've discussed this, agreed that it was easier to get on and off the bow than the stern. Of course, there are exceptions, but if your boat is not easily controlled astern, going in bow first is the answer. Another point to consider is that in some marinas there are outcrops of boulders at the base of the pontoons which can just catch a rudder, but which are well below the level of the bow.

Whether you moor bow-to or stern-to, you will need a strong pair of rubber gloves to pick up the mooring line from the pontoon and take it to the other end of the boat. It is not just that the ropes are usually very dirty, but that shellfish and all sorts can live on them, so it is easy to cut your hand if you don't use gloves. Such cuts are likely to go septic very quickly.

Chapter Eighteen

Why we chose a Junk Rig

THERE ARE many advantages to the modern junk rig, particularly the superjunk rigs, and having tried two different ones I was most impressed. It is true that the junk rigs of 20 years ago do not sail well to windward, but the modern ones are very different, sailing well on all points of sail. We have certainly never regretted our decision to buy a boat with this rig. The main advantages are:

- The speed and ease of reefing and unreefing, which enables you to adjust the amount of sail in a minute or two. Generally, you can reef and unreef on any point of sail. On many days, we reefed three or four times;
- With six or seven panels on each sail, it is almost always possible to set the precise amount of sail for the wind strength;
- If you need to lower the sails completely, you just pay out the halyards from the cockpit and down they come;

The Leisurely Route to the Med

- Junk rig boats sail faster down wind than boats with conventional rigs because a greater proportion of the sail is higher up, where the wind speed is greater, and because they are stable. Also, the boom is light, so an accidental gybe does not damage the rigging or the crew—it usually happens slowly because there isn't the big mass of the boom to hurl it across;
- They are also easy to tack—you just put the helm over, without any heaving on sheets and winches;
- The sails of the superjunk rig can be moved fore and aft relative to the mast. When running before the wind they are moved forward so that the centre of pressure is nearer the centre of the boat, reducing the tendency to roll;
- You can motor with the fully battened sail raised when there is no wind and it will not flog; it just sits waiting for the wind, catching the slightest breeze;
- With the flexible battens and other innovations, boats with the superjunk rig can sail as close to the wind as Bermudan rigged boats with similar hulls, and sail very well with the wind on the beam;
- The absence of standing rigging is a boon in the lack of noise in high winds, and in reduced running costs and stress on the mast and rigging;
- The motion of a junk rig boat is rather smoother from that of a Bermudan rig;
- The junk rig is low-tech—a failure can be repaired easily almost anywhere. Although some of the ropes are usually pre-stretched, they are all of small diameter and lightly stressed. With a hole in one panel of the sail, the boat can still sail without ripping the whole sail to shreds.

Disadvantages:
- It takes longer to raise the sails than with a conventional rig;
- The junk rig seems complicated owing to the large number of ropes required, but few of these need to be adjusted once the sails are set.

Specification - *Zefka*

Brewer Junk rig schooner built in Canada 1983, major refit in 1994
L.O.A. 32ft 8in (9.96m)
L.W.L. 28ft 0in (8.53m)
Beam   10ft 4in (3.15m)
Draft   5ft 3in (1.6 m)
Displacement 6.25 tons
Ballast 2.5 tons
Ted Brewer design, with aluminium hull, deck and coachroof
Long fin keel, skeg hung rudder
Aft cockpit
Four berths in two cabins
Sunbird Marine superjunk rig, tan sails, aluminium alloy masts
Mainsail 350 ft^2 (32m^2); foresail 265ft^2 (24.6m^2);
Total 615 ft^2 (56.6m^2)
Bukh 24hp diesel engine and saildrive
Fuel tank 180 litres
Fresh water tanks 400 litres
Electric winch for halyards, electric anchor windlass
Anchors: one 45lb CQR, one 50lb Brittany spade-type,
one 15lb Danforth type kedge anchor
Autohelm Autopilot 4000T
Autohelm log, speed and depth gauges
Navtex 4 weather information receiver
Shipmate 5800 GPS
Sailor Compact VHF radio
Avon four-man liferaft
Avon Redstart inflatable dinghy
Jonbuoy retrieval unit
Spinflo Nelson gas cooker
Rinnai water heater system to sink, wash basin and shower
Lectrasan toilet system (switches to a sea toilet as required)
Radio/cassette player with remote loudspeakers
Supercool fridge built into coolbox
3.2Amp solar panel
Detachable 8Amp battery charger

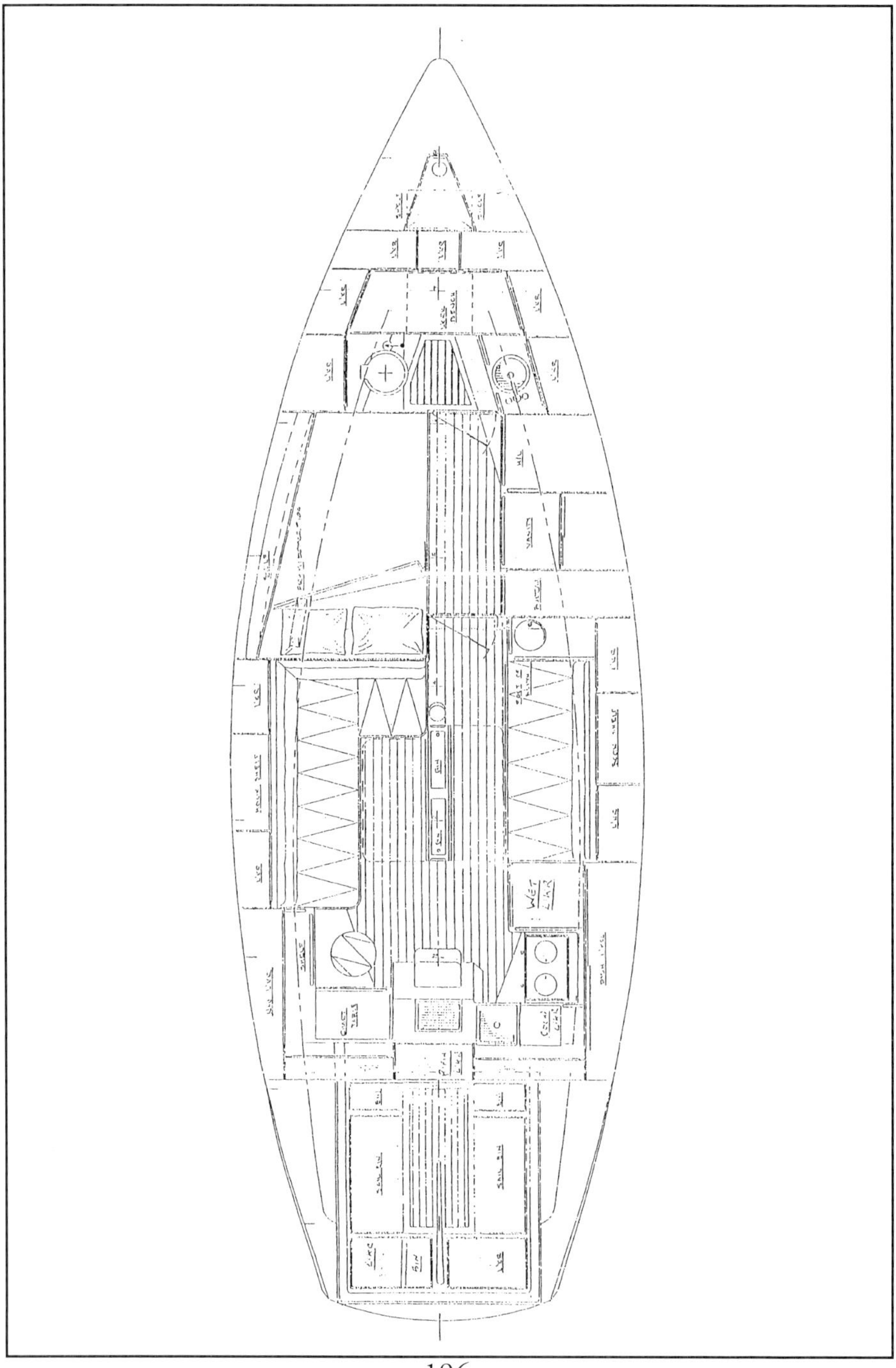

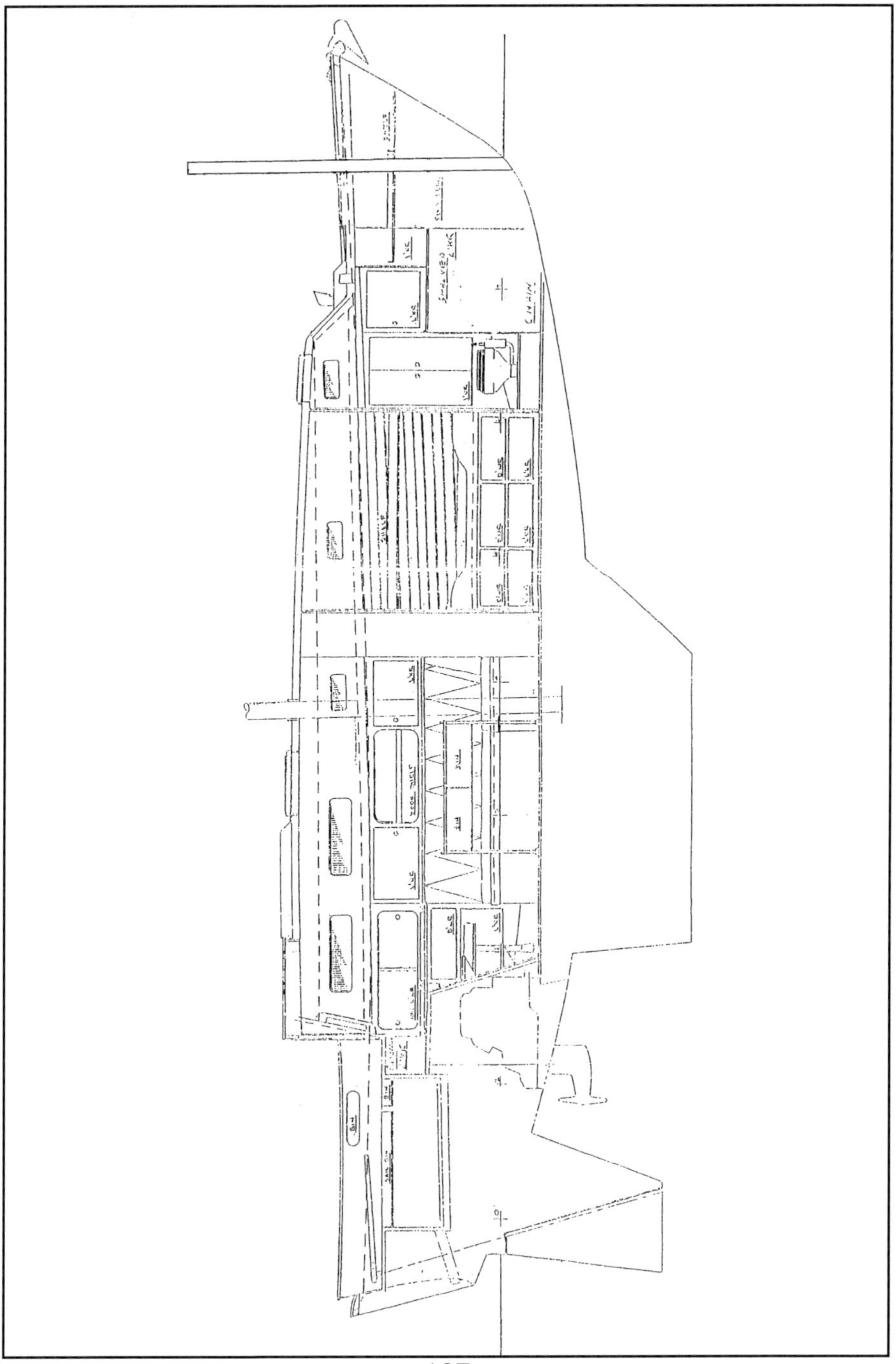

Chapter Nineteen

Spare parts, special equipment and provisions

WE TOOK quite a few essential spare parts, but since we intended to remain sailing in the EU, we did not take the huge amount of spares people used to take a decade ago. I followed the recommendations of Rod Heikell in 'Mediterranean Cruising Handbook' for engine spares and other essentials. We had also arranged with Mountbatten Boathouse at Plymouth Yacht Haven that they would send out anything we needed as quickly as they could. The equipment listed is principally what we thought was necessary not just for this voyage, but also for the first year or so the boat would be in the Med. Some items were on the boat when we bought her.

Engine spares
1 injector
1 full gasket set
2 water pump impellers

2 oil filters
2 primary fuel filters
2 secondary fuel filters
Hoses for cooling system
2 engine anodes
1 fan belt
1 solenoid to shut off fuel supply
1 old fuel lift pump

Other equipment
Grease gun
1 seacock
1 saildrive anode
1 saildrive retaining screw
1 three-blade propeller
Disc anodes for attachment to hull
Courtesy flags for France, Portugal and Spain
A 12mm (1/2in) bore hosepipe of food quality, 20 metres in length
A variety of quick-release hose fittings for fresh water supply, male and female. Hose clips are also needed in some marinas.
A mains electric cable with a standard three-pin marina connection, and a short extension with a French two-pin plug.
We found that the three-pin plug was used in most marinas, and where a different one is used, they either make you rent one to pay for your electricity or they lend you one. An extension lead, to double the length of the cable from 20 to 40 metres may be needed in some yards, but not normally in marinas themselves—unless someone has blown the trip on the nearest electrical outlet, which seems to happen quite often.
Underwater goggles, in case you need to free a rope from the propeller, or just to see how the anchor is lying.
The usual assortment of flares, life jackets, first aid kit, tools, warps, buckets, nuts, bolts, shackles, seizing wire and other paraphernalia found on most boats.
You will spend many days at sea, so good seating in the cockpit will make your days more comfortable. The coamings of most yachts are not very

Spare parts, special equipment and provisions

comfortable, nor is it pleasant leaning against the guard rail for several hours, so we recommend some of those cushions which combine seats and backrests. A simple cockpit table is also worth having.

Provisions

Because we are vegans, our provision list will differ from those of meat-eaters, but is included to show the sort of volume needed. One of the advantages of the vegetarian diet is that beans, either dehydrated or tinned, are one of the main foodstuffs. Of course, these have long shelf lives, and do not take up much room.

We took enough tofu to last us for the whole voyage—which it did—because it is available long-life as well as fresh, and we did not expect to be able to find it on the way. Once under way, we shopped principally for vegetables, fruit and wine, and once in Spain for beans and pulses as well. We also took some special ingredients that are usually found in health food shops only. We did find a health food shop in almost every major port in Spain, some good and some very poor.

Our cooking utensils consist of a frying pan, two saucepans and a small pressure cooker, which is ideal for cooking beans, and some oven dishes. We chose the Nelson Spinflo cooker largely because the oven has a good thermostat, which is essential for all but basic cooking. It has performed very well.

The Leisurely Route to the Med

Protein foods
Beans and pulses, 16 tins, 5 pkts
Tofu, long-life, 12 blocks
TVP (soya protein) dehydrated, 1 pkt
Hummus, 6 tins and 2 dehydrated pkts
Bean meals, 2 tins
Sosmix, 2 pkts
Nut roast mix, 3 pkts
Mixed nuts

Grains, etc
Pasta, 4 pkts
Grains (rice, etc), 6 pkts
Cereals, 1 pkt
Oatcakes, 2 pkts
Flour, 2 pkts
Wholemeal bread mix, 6 pkts

Vegetables
Tins, 6
Tomato puree, 2 tubes
Pasta sauce, 3 jars
Soups (individual), 28 pkts

Fruit
Various fruits, 6 tins
Dried apricots, 1 pkt
Dried figs, 1 pkt
Sultanas, 1 pkt
Raisins, 1 pkt

Spreads
Tahini, 3 jars
Peanut butter, 2 jars
Yeast extract, 2 jars
Spicy bean spread, 2 jars
Various pâtés, 5 jars
Marmalade, 3 jars
Jam, 1 jar

Stocks, sauces, etc
Egg-free mayonnaise, 1 jar
Engevita nutritional yeast, 2 containers
Vecon vegetable stock concentrate, 2 jars
Dijon mustard, 1 jar
Olive oil, 1 litre
Parmazano dairy-free powder, 2 pkts
Tamari sauce, 1 bottle
Tomato ketchup, 1 bottle
Date syrup, 1 bottle
Wine vinegar, 1 bottle

Drinks
Orange juice, 8 cartons
Soya milk, 24 litres
UHT milk, 2 litres
NoCaf drink powder, 4 jars
Nescafe, decaffeinated, 1 small jar
Coffeemate, 1 jar
Coffee filter papers, 1 pkt
Filter coffee, 1 pkt
Tea bags, 80
Water, 10 litres
Wine, 3 bottles (to keep us going at the beginning of the voyage!)

The Leisurely Route to the Med

Other
Digestive biscuits, 2 pkts
Ginger biscuits, 1 pkt
Salted peanuts, 2 pkts

Health /medical
First aid kit
Aspirin
Vitamin C, 1000mg, 120 tablets
Multi-vitamin & mineral, 240 tablets
Stugeron, 1 pkt
Insect repellant, 1 aerosol
Strong suntan lotion (Nos. 15 & 25)
After-sun lotion

Toiletries
Soap tablets, 2
Toothpaste, 2 tubes
Toilet rolls, 8
Shampoo, etc

Cleaning materials
Automatic washing liquid, 1 litre containers, 2
Fabric conditioner, 1/2 litre
Hand-washing liquid, 1/2 litre
Washing up liquid, 1 litre containers, 2
J-cloths, 25
Clothes pegs
Washing-up brush
Kitchen rolls, 2

Spare parts, special equipment and provisions

Sundries
Electric travellers' kettle
Electric hand blender
Plastic food containers
Plastic food bags
Mending kit
Sunglasses, Polaroid (These help to see rocks and seaweed on the seabed)
Batteries, LR6, 12
Notebooks, small, 4
Camera and film
Camcorder and cassettes
Music cassettes
Cash (A deposit is needed in many marinas for keys to the toilets or other equipment, and they usually require cash, so you do need to carry the equivalent of £30-40 in cash)
Travellers' cheques
Credit cards
Passports
E111s
Boat documents

Reference books
French, Portuguese and Spanish dictionaries
MacMillan Reeds Nautical Almanac or Looseleaf Almanac
North Biscay Pilot
Biscay Spain Pilot
Atlantic Spain and Portugal Pilot
Mediterranean: Costa del Sol & Cost Blanca
Mediterranean Cruising Handbook by Rod Heikell
Boatowner's Mechanical & Electrical Manual by Nigel Calder
Charts: we used Admiralty charts which seemed to be the best for such a large area. Most were 1:200,000, but a few were more detailed, including some showing ports on various parts of the coast, which were invaluable. Spanish charts do not seem to be so good, nor readily available, but there are some good French charts.

The Leisurely Route to the Med

Paperbacks: A selection of paperbacks will help while away the time should you get stuck in a harbour waiting for the weather to break. In quite a few marinas they have a small library where you can exchange your old books for others.

Books of interest

'Practical Junk Rig' by Blondie Hasler and Jock McLeod
'Voyaging on a Small Income' by Annie and Peter Hill (well-known junk-rig cruisers)
'Brazil and Beyond' by Annie and Peter Hill
'Sell up and Sail' by Bill and Laurel Cooper
'The Self-Sufficient Sailor' by Lin and Larry Pardey
'Cost-Conscious Cruiser' by Lin and Larry Pardey
'Heavy Weather Sailing' by Adlard Coles (if you want to frighten yourself!)

For information on junk rigs contact:
 The Junk Rig and Advanced Cruising Rig Association
373 Hunts Pond Rd
Titchfield Common
Fareham
Hants PO14 4PB
Tel: 01329 842613
Fax: 01329 315232
Hon. Secretary: Robin Blain

Pauline Drury and John Hartley were both introduced to sailing in dinghies. Pauline was in Fife, and she found it very cold and rather unpleasant, while John was in Japan, where he sailed a dinghy for several years. However, once he tried a yacht, he knew that was his kind of sailing.

Therefore, when he returned from Japan in 1988, he did some sailing courses and bought a MacWester Wight ketch which he sailed for four years from Guernsey around the Channel Islands and to the French coast. Then, he returned to the UK. After having lived in Scotland for 18 years, Pauline gave up her horse and a full-time job teaching in Special Education to live in Devon with John.

As time permitted, Pauline was able to sail more and found that compared with dinghy sailing, cruising in a yacht off the south coast was a welcome change, but still very cold at times.

John bought *Zefka,* a Brewer junk rig schooner in 1998, and sailed it with Pauline for a season from Plymouth before they headed down to the Mediterranean where they now sail whenever they can. Now they are both keen to explore the Med—sailing in warm waters, the leisurely way.

John trained in the motor industry, and has worked as a professional writer, principally involved with technology and manufacture, for 30 years. He has had 15 books published.

Pauline still teaches disabled children, but on a supply basis, which makes it possible to take long holidays during term time. The voyage to the Mediterranean was one of exploration—much more interesting than cruising locally.